To: Jodi a Jay's Mommy B.J & Daddy Doug

MY FIRST CHRISTMAS

From: Chelsea Mommy Cw

CATHIE GRAY

ISBN: 1508492859
ISBN-13: 9781508492856

DEDICATION

This body of work is dedicated, to My Beautiful Chelsea Alexis (Davis) Gray, which I lost, 8-7-14. She is 'one of a kind', and will always be the first, of my 3 beautiful children and the heartbeat of Angela, Tre and I. SHE makes our rhythm complete. My book is also dedicated, to My Son, My Rock, Tre Davis. You are the man I look up to and am so immensely proud of, for all that you do, did, and will do. You are my 'Leading Man' until and even after, I take my last breathe. This book is also dedicated to My Darling princess Angela and to all the beauty that is you. Never change who and how you are. You truly are amazing, and you make Chelsea proud every day. Your smile, face, voice, and mind is a force, to be reckoned with and is truly unmatched. **C**-helsea, **A**-ngela, and **T**-re=**CAT**! I'm nothing without them!! Mommy Loves You Always & Infinity & Beyond!!

CONTENTS

ACKNOWLEDGMENTS

I'd like to acknowledge Chelsea's Daddy, Robert Gray. Thank you for loving 'our girl' the way you did. I'd like to acknowledge 'Squad, MHG, Flinstoners' for their constant support of My Son and The KCA Movement. I'd like to acknowledge Vikki Hankins, the publisher of VMH Magazine & Producer of the Vikki Hankins Show, for allowing me, to remember my love of writing, just a few months before I lost My Chelsea. I'd like to acknowledge Romi G. for being a 'vessel' during this journey; To all of you that have joined The KCA Movement, as well as Special friends that have supported The KCA Movement's bracelets fundraisers like Kris Bennett, DeeDee Procaccini of Big Dawgs 2 & Tin Cup, Pamela Farmer, Linda Hansen Buie, and Shapprell, Patrick & Destiny Dallas, of Top Bodies Fitness. I'd like to also thank all of the genuine friends that expressed concern, encouragement, love, and support during this tumultuous journey. Please know that you are all appreciated.

1 DEAR DIARY

Dear Diary,

It's December 24, 2014. To the world, it is Christmas Eve. As everyone makes sure that their Christmas list is complete and their Holiday spirit is at an all-time optimum level. The world appears vastly different for me. With their Christmas lights beaming and meticulously arranged decorations, they sing their carols of delight and wrap their presents, while I search for strength, to inflate my lungs, after every single exhalation. My To-Do List isn't gift shopping, wrapping, and masterfully selected recipe ingredients. Fighting back the tears, inhaling, exhaling, controlling organ quivering, all have risen to the top of tasks for me, this day.

This cheerful holiday, with all of its Jolly, Merry, Happy festive introductions, is far from any of those things, in my fragmented heart and wood chippered soul.

'Joy to The World' they say. 'Peace for *all* mankind' they say. My derision and disparagement of this bliss, consumes my inner voids, as I strategically engage the universe in my game of 'hide and go cry'. I can't see brightness. Period. I can't conceive jovial festive *anything*. Period. The one thing I want for Christmas, my Birthday, Mother's Day, Valentine's Day, New Year's Day, and all other gift giving prospective occasions, is MY CHELSEA BACK. Period.

All of the lights, may as well go black and be obscured to my mortal eye, because this 'Zombie' doesn't appreciate or conceive their colors or flash or glimmer or purpose, this time. Zombie, you ask? Isn't that what the walking dead are called these days? Moving, skin-wrapped, body parts lacking a cadenced heartbeat or pulse that subsists, without substance, of any value, all the while, 'sleep deprived undertaking' daily since, August 7, 2014. Yes, that's me. That is what it feels like this day. How can the world be in the midst of record-breaking merriment and gaiety tonight, this year, without My Chelsea in it? How can I? That isn't a feat, challenge, or quest that any spirit, top shelf or otherwise, can assist me with.

November 3, 1992, was the first happiest day, of my life!! Doctor Goss said "It's a Girl", and the only one word I could muster, to utter, after 37 hours of labor. My pregnancy had been riddled with intractable nausea and 32 visits, to the hospital emergency room, those 9 months.

Seeing her eyes, "SUNSHINE" was all that came out, when I laid my exhausted eyes on her beauty at 1:37 a.m. that unforgettable November morning. The Longwood Florida Hospital staff even wrote 'Sunshine Davis' on her paperwork, until I corrected them. Chelsea Alexis is her name, I revealed later that morning, after the actual sun had risen. I hadn't just came up with it, I'd known her name since I was 12, and now at 21, I held my 'real life' Baby doll. I expected, that day in 1992, the same thing I expected on the morning of August 7th 2014, TO NOT KNOW HER DATE OF DEATH, because I'd never wanted to know life again without her!!

Here I sit. Christmas Eve 2014 and I still have 3 children. Two, Angela and Tre, that I can hold and now, one that will hold me. Those were her words. To Me. From beyond. Those words became my lifeline. That one phrase, that one sentence was now the reason I would buy 3 tickets, to the show, sadly not 4. Those words would be the reason I am alive, this Christmas Eve, to gift you, with my experience. Selfishly, I scream GIVE HER BACK!!! Unselfishly I give to you, all that she has given to me.

This book, inspired by her, will be my Christmas present to you, TO THE WORLD. It is wrapped and taped with the greatest pain known to a human. Not just a loss, but the LOSS OF A CHILD!!! She was 21, she may as well have been 21 months old, 21 days old, or 21 minutes old. She was MY baby. MINE. Our hearts beat in sync, so my cardiac song will forever be offbeat, off key. Like a song, with no bass line, 2 profound verses, My Tre and My Angela, 2 perfect verses, but never a complete song, without a bass line, without My Chelsea.

'When a mother bestows her name, on a child, it reveals her hope' they say. My Chelsea Alexis was named, for the beautiful princess girly-girl denoted, by her first name, with strength attached in her bold middle name. I knew she would be both, strong and beautiful. The non-ethnic derivation in her name, would make it hard for her, to be pre-judged, by name alone. She would at least not be stereotypically pigeon holed, when her resume appeared on a future fax machine. Too bad the world was such a cruel place that I had birthed my royal fragile prize possession into. (If you want to know more about her death and cause, there is an explosive tell-all available on Amazon.com called SAFE by D.D.T. Gray)(It hurt SOOO bad, the death of her, caused the death of me and the rage gave birth to D.D.T. Gray)

My Holi-days are Hollow Days.

You stream lights, your Christmas lights. So many lights, yet if you used them like counter beads, back before we had calculators, to count the pieces my heart is in, you would run out of lights before you came up with a number. I'd like to find any light. You anxiously await waking tomorrow morning, Christmas day. Every morning, tomorrow morning included, since August 7th is warfare in my DNA. My eyes open, an immediate reconciliation, an accounting, of my kids, creates havoc, in every system, in my body. Tomorrow morning won't be any different, it will be worse. I will wake, with a new emotion, seldom, if ever, experienced, Jealousy. I will be Jealous, of all you, jealous because *all* of your children *will* come down your stairs.

My Holi-days are Hollow Days.

Dear Diary,

12-25-2014 Christmas Day- My First Christmas without My Chelsea

My eyes open. *"Where are my children?"* My waking thought, for the last 21 years. Angela is with her Daddy. Clinton and the Barnes family are so lucky to have that ray of sunshine this morning. Tre is an adult, 256 miles away, probably sleeping in. I sent his gifts early. *MY CHELSEA, MY SWEET SWEET CHELSEA, MY TWIN, I WANT TO PICK UP THIS PHONE AND TELL HER IM ON MY WAY! WHERE WILL I DRIVE? SHE ISNT AT HER APARTMENT!! SHE IS GONE CAT!! CHELSEA DIED CAT!!*

I hate THAT ROAD she lived and DIED on. SUNRISE Boulevard, they call it? I should definitely protest, insisting for Broward County to change the name of it! It now seems like some sick twisted oxymoron, poking fun at me. *OH MY GOD, HOW WILL I GO ON, WITHOUT My CHELSEA? MY BEAUTIFUL TWIN? OH DEAR GOD!!*

As soon as I can feel my legs, I will go and stare, in the mirror, until I see her face. I want to wake up from this. Hell, I am awake. *OH MY GOD, MY CHELSEA!!!* I can't feel my hands. Breathe Cat. My hands have to be here. Try to make a fist. Ok, breathe Cat. Dummy, exhale. Inhale. Yes Idiot, exhale again. Chelsea is going to call today. *NO SHE ISNT.* We won't shop this year. We didn't shop this year. SHE will always have that title, My FAVORITE Shopper. SHE dressed me!! She had an eye, for selecting my clothes as if they were tailor made and she herself, had drawn the sketches, for the most elite fashion designer. That Girl has fashion sense. *That Beautiful girl HAD fashion sense, Cat.*

MY ANGEL IS GONE!! MY ANGEL. YES, NOW SHE JUST HAS THE WINGS TO MATCH!! Silly Sad Mommy. *OH MY GOD, I WANT HER, TO WALK THROUGH THIS DOOR!!*

I can feel a few of my fingers now. I'm squeezing my right hand tighter, I think. Tingling. Ok, tingling is good. I can feel my right leg now. Breathe Cat. And yes, exhale this time too.

I swear, that automatic trigger in your respiratory system that trades the carbon monoxide for oxygen, snapped into tiny pieces, the night of August 7th, when I pulled up to her apartment building and saw all of those people and police cars with their flashing lights. Nothing is automatic anymore. I can feel my left foot now, it is still there. *I WANT MY CHELT. I CANT SEE. THE PAIN IS BLINDING ME!!*

The morning's REALIZATION PAIN, that is always present, like your words 'Good Morning', BASHES me!! My soul is thwarted, with a greeting, from the universe of devastation!! I wake into this nightmare every morning since August 7th. Or shall I say August 11th. I didn't sleep for 4 days straight, trying to get to the bottom of what had happened to MY Precious Girl. This AM caricature, is presented, with the most unpretentious action, on my behalf, of my eyelids simply coming apart.

It is CHRISTMAS morning to you all. *MERRY??? I THINK NOT!!* My soul screams. You will wake and say Merry Christmas. *I LITERALLY CANT EVEN SEE!!* OH, the puddled TEARS, my soul is flooded. I can't corral the floodgates this Christmas morning, of yours.
YES, YOURS, I AM GIVING CHRISTMAS BACK TO YOU ALL!! THERE IS NO MERRY ANYTHING, WITHOUT MY CHELT IN IT!! This lake of underwater blindness, latitude and longitude coordinates of my eye sockets, will only exacerbate this morning, this Christmas Morning of theirs, of the worlds', *if you don't sit up Cat.* I try to reason with myself. Reasoning isn't working. The PAIN is insuperable!!

It is the same insupportable, arduous, penetrating greeting as yesterday, and all days, all 136 days, all 3,264 hours, 195,840 minutes, back to August 11th!!

The world's Christmas lights, Christmas trees, immaculate yard nativity scenes, all of their Holiday parties and record breaking presents purchased and wrapped, at their planned gift wrapping gatherings, *ISN'T MAKING THIS, MY CHELSEA'S ABSENCE, ANY LESS DEVASTATING TO UNWRAP!!*

This pain bashes my soul every morning. PAIN is simply broadcasted like the words they utter 'good morning' EVERY SINGLE MORNING, SINCE.

Close your eyes Cat. Use your eyelids like pain 'windshield wipers', Cat. Tears are streaming down, into the grottos of my ears. I can't sit up yet. I need two functional hands for that. I have sensation, in only 4, of my 10 fingers, so far. Squeeze your fists tighter. *You can do this. COME ON CAT. CHELSEA WANTS YOU TO!!* Breathe, hell inhale, count to 3 now. Exhale. Inhale and try to count to 5 this time. With all the strength I can muster, I Exhale.

7

Counting out loud 1, 2, 3; I can't make it to 5 yet. Not enough strength in my soul, WITHOUT HER to fully expand my lungs. But you have to, Cat. Chelsea has a purpose. A greater purpose. Chelsea gave me a purpose. I gave her life at 21. She died and gave me life during her 21st year. There they are. 10 fingers. Breathe deeper. Exhale. OK I have 2 legs, feeling in 1 foot, half functional lungs at this point, feeling in 8 fingers so far, my stomach is in knots.

Was I in a car wreck, last night? 'Their' Christmas Eve, in my dream? Not wearing a seatbelt? Was I thrown from the vehicle, through the windshield, in the middle of rush hour traffic on I-95, and pummeled by cars- trucks and semis, before I fell off the overpass into another lane of fast driving cars, in this overpopulated Broward County? *NO CAT, CHELSEA DIED. THAT'S YOUR ANSWER. CHELSEA DIED!!*

I chant my mantra, in the feeblest voice, which is all that I can muster at this time, this moment: *I HAVE 3 CHILDREN. TWO I CAN HOLD, ONE THAT WILL HOLD ME NOW!!*

My heart needs to be hooked up to electrical stimulation, I just know it. I need an aggregation of strength, from somewhere, to get up and open this door and *CHELSEA NEEDS TO BE ON THE OTHER SIDE!! SHE WON'T BE, CAT. YOU HAD 21 YEARS. YOU DON'T HAVE 21 YEARS PLUS THIS CHRISTMAS MORNING THAT THE WORLD REJOICES. 21 YEARS.* That's it.

Like all time-stamped events, it began on November 3rd in 1992 and ENDED AUGUST 7th, two thousand and fourteen. I spell that year out, to see if my brain is working. It is shorting like a short circuiting closed-caption monitor, at this moment. I know CHELSEA is gone, but all that is running across the bottom, of this mental monitor is CAT CALL HER!! GO TO SUNRISE BLVD, MAYBE SHE IS THERE!! MAYBE I HAVE BEEN IN ONE LONG DREAM, ONE LONG NIGHTMARE, IT STARTED August 7th, in my dream-world and ended just now, when my eyes opened!! Exhale Cat. You know that *that* isn't true. SHE IS GONE!!

You know Cat. YOU KNOW YOU KNOW!! IF YOU PULL YOUR HAND, FROM UNDER THE COVER, AND there is a bracelet on your hand that says THE KCA MOVEMENT, it means SHE IS GONE!! Breathe, Cat. Breathe. YOU KNOW YOU KNOW!! As if I could still have an ounce of a chance of making it untruthful, I slowly slide my hand from under the covers......
THE BRACELET IS THERE!! Gasping for air again.

Sit up Cat. Streams of Tears heavily coursing down, to my breast now.

The same breast that fed her beautiful face, for 2 years. Yes, 2 years. I was told, back then, it would guarantee a stronger immune system. I would do anything for HER. For Him too. Yes, they are only 18 months apart, so for 6 months I breastfed 2 children. Chelsea and Tre sometimes simultaneously.

A small sneer comes across my tear roofed face.

That vision, that image of looking into my 2 beautiful babies faces, as they smile up at me, each one suckling from a breast of mine, they had each claimed, as their own. But Tre and his instantaneous love of 'YUM-YUM', he called these breast feedings, would always have to try to reach, and at least, lay a hand on Chelsea's pre-selected 'booby' of mine, that her petite angelic face, had claimed. Meanwhile, Tre was extracting milk like a NFL football player with a straw in his Gatorade, at halftime of the Super bowl, with the Miami Dolphins up by 14.

Stupid mental insertion there, I start to think. I love my Dolphins. Guess my humor button still works, Dolphins are not in the Super bowl and probably won't be soon. I hadn't missed a game of football since I was 5 years old, until this year. Football season was in its 7th weeks, before I could even remember which day of the week was Sunday. The calendar was regular, but all I saw when I looked at it, was one more day since My 'Chelt' was gone!

BREATHE CAT!! If it was a possibility, I would trade my idealistic dream of coaching the Miami Dolphins, if my phone would just ring and BABYGIRL CHELT, with that breathtaking million dollar smiling photo attached to her phone number, in my phone, would just scroll across the screen!! I pick up the phone, no missed call, scrolling now, yet no missed or incoming BABYGIRL CHELT appears in my call log. Wheeewwwwww, I exhale, just breathe Cat.

I would even give up both my legs and one of my arms for *that* phone call from her. I'd only ask to keep one arm, so I can squeeze her and never let her go again, just to stop this feeling, now, that I have felt it.

Ok. Ok. Ok. Cat none of that is realistic. BREATHE.

Breathing a little more regulated now. Both feet are here. My heart is misfiring, as it catches up, to itself. Stomach already in a knot, so do a crunch motion and put your feet, on the floor, Cat. Both of them, Cat. You have to. CHELSEA wants you to. TRE and ANGELA need you to. Both feet planted. One long deep exhale. I stand....hiss, *they said 'and to all a good night'. Good night? No Good night. No good night since August 7, 2014.*

OK, I have to put right foot, in front of left foot and repeat. All body parts inventoried. This morning, their Christmas Morning, same off-kilter mechanical misalignment every morning, *is never going to be the same without My 'Chelt'!! Period!!* Everything is here. Yet it feels like I have nothing. Nothing without HER, that is.

It's like a pretty car, but only one cable to the battery is there. Tre would be THE cable, Angela would be the posts that he is holding on to so tightly. My CHELT IS THE BATTERY. *THAT POWERFUL GIRL IS THE BATTERY. Don't cry again, Cat. It won't change it. Don't Cry. You just got your eyesight back. Try your pain windshield wipers again. Come on Cat. You have to, Cat.*

As if on speaker phone, I now hear: **"Come on Mommy"** SHE would say. "Ok, Mommy coming", I reply out loud. "MOMMY COMING". *Breathe. Just Breathe Cat.* She speaks again. I swear, I hear her voice saying:

"YOU HAVE 3 CHILDREN MOMMY. YOU WILL ALWAYS HAVE 3 CHILDREN MOMMY. THAT NUMBER DIDN'T CHANGE TODAY MOMMY. IM RIGHT HERE MOMMY. PLEASE DON'T CRY MOMMY. Breathe Mommy. Breathe Mommy. Breathe Mommy."
"OK CHELT. OK. I'm breathing." *I know, I know. Ok. I'm up. wheeeeewwwwwwwww. I don't know how, but I will, baby. I will go on and do all that you predetermined me to do. I will make you proud. Tre is making you proud. Angela is making you proud. Mommy won't give up, this morning.*
Ok. Ok. Ok. I'm up. I'm ok.
I will call Angela and call Tre as soon as I don't sound like this. Like I just gave myself a shower, with that outburst, of stomach-originating gut wrenching tears, heaved, from the deepest muscular region of my core. I'm ok Baby. I know you got me. I know. I'm up, you can rest, and I'll get moving soon.
All body parts accounted for, just interspersed, with red eyes now, and a runny nose, but hey that's morning.
*Ok Cat. I have 3 children. I have 3, Three, Tres', 1-2-3 Children. OK. I got it....*more mental tricks and coaching needed, *this* morning.

The world is smiling and taking pictures and their children everywhere are giggling and opening presents and they are having a MERRY Christmas morning…*OK,(* I whisper*)*, as the tears start, to gain momentum again.

I can't see her with my eyes open, but my DNA has a soundtrack again, that interrupts my train of thought just as I am spiraling down into envying all of you, this day. 'Your' Christmas, with all of your children present and accounted for, sitting on your living room floor, around your punctiliously selected ornament medley. As I'm plunging further, into this jealousy anguish-filled whirlpool, I hear:

"It's Ok Mommy. It's OK. They are happy. That's Ok. Let them be happy, Mommy. You stay inside today. You're OK Mommy. You have 3 children. 'Merry Christmas' they will shout, from the rooftops, don't hurt over that, Momma. You will get through this one, like you got through every other day, since August 7th, one freaking moment at a time. They will never understand, that this has been the longest-orbiting-shortest-longest nightmare, time wise, of your life.
They don't know, that it seems like days last for a week. They don't know you are now living, in minute-increments not hours, certainly not 24 hours at a time, but 1,440 minutes a day. They don't know all at the same time, each minute, seems like, one minute past *THE* moment you got that call from My Tre-Tre, saying YOUR 'Chelt' was gone. They don't know Mommy.
God, that had to be soooooo hard, for Him. To pick up the phone and make that call, Momma. AFTER FINDING OUT, ON FACEBOOK no doubt, people. My Poor TRE TRE!!

It goes silent again. The sound, of her voice, in my head, paused. It is Just Me and My Pain now, again.

Ok. Ok. OK. I have 3 children. (if you care to know how that devastating phone-call, unveiling, and all the moments following that went, including my arriving on the scene, fighting to get to her, never being allowed to. It is all in my first raw gritty expose' SAFE by D.D.T. Gray.(www.createspace.com/4969825) If you read it, you will understand so much more, from this experience.) She didn't die, of natural causes. *Ok. Ok. Ok. Don't think about that now, Cat.*

Her voice interrupts, that shattering train of thought, as I close my eyes a few times quicker, as if to expedite utilization of the tear wipers. Lastly, I keep my eyes closed, as if to auto-tune the settings of the Chelsea soundtrack in my DNA, I am yearning to hold down the button marked PLAY, when I hear:

"I have a Purpose Mama. A GRAND Purpose. You have an even GREATER PURPOSE MAMA. I want YOU, to save all the other 'Chelsea's', MAMA. YOU WON'T BE REPLACING ME MAMA. YOU have 3 children she says. YOU WILL ALWAYS HAVE 3 CHILDREN MOMMY, plus the thousands I gave YOU TO, in this now life-changing, (my mind says daunting) task. I HAVE A GIFT FOR THE WORLD, MAMA. You won't go to the store and purchase this one. You won't wrap it, in a conventional sense, Mama. YOU WILL WRITE IT!!

I WILL GUIDE YOU, MAMA. YOU AND I WILL BE THE SPIRIT OF CHRISTMAS AFTER ALL MAMA.

WE WILL GIVE THEM A GIFT, ONE THAT WILL TRULY 'KEEP ON GIVING'.

I NEED YOU TO NOT GIVE UP CATHIE GRAY.

OUR GIFT WILL GIVE LIFE TO THE 'INVISIBLE' ONES. I WAS AN INVISIBLE ONE, MOMMA. DON'T CRY NOW. OUR GIFT WILL SAVE THEM MAMA.

THEY WONT RECEIVE THEIR GIFT THIS CHRISTMAS, THIS CHRISTMAS IS OUR CHRISTMAS, MOMMY. JUST YOU AND ME.

BUT OUR GIFT WILL CHANGE ALL OF THEIR OTHER CHRISTMASES MOMMA. IT WILL BE LIKE A GIFT FROM EVERYONE THEY HAVE LOVED AND LOST. WE WILL HELP EVERYONE, MAMA. TRUST ME.

I KNOW YOU DON'T LIKE NOT BEING ABLE TO CONTROL ANYTHING. I KNOW YOU WANNA PUSH ONE OF YOUR BUTTONS AND BRING ME BACK MOMMY. BUT YOU LOOKING AT IT WRONG. IM RIGHT HERE. YOU DON'T NEED TO WAIT FOR A CALL OR CLICK ON MY PICTURE AND SIT THERE COUNTING RINGS, TO HEAR MY VOICE MOMMY. IM RIGHT HERE.

YOU ALREADY MADE ME PROUD. I KNOW IT HURT YOU SO VERY BAD, TO WRITE SAFE BY D.D.T. GRAY. I STILL LOVE HOW YOU CAME UP WITH THAT NAME, OFF MY NICKNAME, (she laughs) I WAS 'DO DAT' to the WORLD. MY OL' GIRL BECAME 'DON'T DO THAT' thus D.D.T. GRAY (MY CHOSEN DADDY'S LAST NAME, OF COURSE.) I LOVE HIM! I LOVE HER! I LOVE YOU, MOMMY! (She laughs again) I KNOW THEY DIDN'T SEE THAT COMING, MOMMY. I even snickered now.

IN THE words of a brilliant, beautiful, strong woman I know, Ya'll, THIS IS NOT THAT!! MY FIRST CHRISTMAS, THIS BOOK,

WILL HELP THEM ALL GET THROUGH, NOT GET OVER, THEIR LOSS. BUT to GET THROUGH, THOSE WORLDWIDE MOMENTOUS OCCASIONS, AFTER LOSING SOMEONE THEY LOVED VERY MUCH!! YOU GOT THIS, MOMMY!! I GOT YOU!! I WILL SHOW YOU THE WAY. YES MOMMA, YOU GAVE BIRTH, TO THE ONE, THAT WILL GIVE THE GIFT THAT KEEPS ON GIVING, MOMMA. YOU DID THAT. YOU MOMMA. DON'T CRY MOMMA. WE, YOU AND ME, WILL, THIS CHRISTMAS, YOUR FIRST CHRISTMAS, GIVE THEM A GIFT FROM US THAT WILL GIVE TO THEM, ALL YEAR-ROUND, MOMMA. YOU HAVE TO BE OK. SAY IT, MOMMA.

As if she was sitting on my bedside, like she had done a 1,000 times, I started to even feel the weight of her draped across me, yet the weight was jumpstarting my malfunctioning bodily systems, as if the other cable was connected, to the battery now. I actually said out loud, *I will Chelsea. I'm ok Chelsea.* **WE GOT THIS MOMMA**!! I heard that last heartening 4 pack of words in my own voice, audibly.

I have to carry out her wishes. I can't let her death be in vain. I CAN NOT!! The KCA Movement (The Keep Chelsea Alive Movement) is here now, it was born August 7th, and I just have to carry this torch.

IT was passed to me by her.

Ok. Ok. Ok, Cat.

Breathing now. Legs, Arms, fingers, toes, Ok. I'll get to the mirror now. MERRY CHRISTMAS, to all. All but me. I want my Chelsea. Ok. Ok. I can do it. I'm Ok. CHELSEA wants me to be ok. Tre & Angela need me to be OK.....After all, I have the massive undertaking of writing a book to the Masses. *I can't let parents walk in my shoes. She said I have to save all the others. I have to give something to the Invisible Ones. Why did she feel invisible? I saw her and all of her beauty and glory,...Ok, Ok, Ok.*

I have to make a difference. CHELSEA PUT IT ON MY TO DO LIST. I won't let her down. I WON'T!! I will this Christmas, My FIRST CHRISTMAS, without My Angel on earth, give you all a gift that will truly, in each and every word KEEP ON GIVING!! SHE SAYS I HAVE TO...I have 3 Children, 2 I can hold, and 1 that will HOLD ME. I FEEL YOU BABY!! Ok...Breathing, Walking, tears lessening to a small stream, now.

"HOLI-DAYS are HOLLOW DAYS"...I whisper out loud

2 QUEST FOR A NEW NORMAL

After reading of what a morning entails for a person, like myself, suffering from a loss of the greatest proportion, a search for functionality, let alone a life of normalcy afterwards, seems unattainable. It isn't just the world's special occasions after the death, of a loved one, that will cause intractable amounts of agony. There is a challenging journey, occurring, for the grieving day by day and moment by moment. This painful expedition is so perplexing. I started to feel I would only be able, to possibly function one day, if I could somehow reside in a very private heavily guarded community. A City exclusively for people that have lost someone that they can't live without. A place, where all of the devastated can live together, on our own planet even, as this quest for normalcy, after this type of agony, makes us feels like aliens, anyway, even in our own homes.

This type of inorganic loss leaves all automatic apparatuses inoperative. If every tool you ever used to do your job, were all of a sudden inaccessible, how would you continue? What would be your next move? How could you successfully execute performance? Your goal of success is now obstructed, with an encircling of impossibility. Moreover, you are not only unable to access all of the skills and experiences, you once possessed, that allowed you to steer through natural life; Simultaneously, you also are now suddenly void of desire and strength to navigate and execute the maze of life. Grief has a way of doing that.

Grief, complicated grief, is accredited with this mounting of inadequacies you now feel. The weight of grief acts as a neutralizer to your life's calibration system. All of life's anchors awry. You find yourself incapable of getting a handle on the rest of your life, after the nonexistence, in a conventional sense, of someone you loved so very much.

To find a way to get a clear understanding of the above, you will need to start to annotate the times you feel that you are without your mental faculties. You are not losing your mind. It is your bearings that are lost. Action is required on your part, with the above acknowledgement, despite the absence of desire, which you are pugnacious to accept.

You are combatting significant next steps, due to your misguided thinking, that by doing so, you are moving away or over the person that you have lost. You have, in essence created the barrier on behalf of your grief waters that is incarcerating your progress. Think about this in light of that, if your goal is to never forget your loved one, how is progress going to change that? Progress in a vehicle, regardless of your starting point is to get to your destination. If your destination is to go to the city of 'Never Let Go of Your Loved One-Ville', then progress only moves you forward, but with that *exact* same destination in sight.

The act of living after suffering a great loss is not a betrayal. It may feel like it at times, as I myself experienced that. I had to realize that my future act of living without my Firstborn Chelsea, had taken on new features and characteristics. Now my life, just as your 'post-loss' life, has to embrace, encompass, and expand the significance of this loved one because they can no longer do it, for themselves. I am not moving on without her, I refuse. You are not moving on without them. Since my goal is to never ever forget her or allow her to be forgotten, living, must now encompass living for and about her, not living beyond her. That now becomes the aim.

Deciding to, defining how, and re-calibrating along the way, with all of the uncontrollable internal pain, will not be the only obstacles we have to encounter. I, like you, will also experience happenstance, with uninvited external pain from 'outsiders'. That too, becomes a part of the very definition of a 'Quest for a New Normal'.

A quest is an expedition, a search, a hunt, a journey, a seeking, of a mission. Please know that that means this 'new normal' isn't a stationary destination. It is a journey that constantly changes. The instability is due to its raw origination and uncontrollable factors. There are many elements, 'effectors', good and bad, influencers, triggers and battles ahead, that makes the stability of this post-loss existence, unreliable.

It would be like hiring the greatest homebuilder, in the world, to build a multi-million dollar home, but the actual lot on which this beautiful structure, is being constructed, is partially-quicksand. Your lost loved one and how you valued them, would be the multi-million dollar structure in this analogy. The shakiness, of your post-loss existence, coupled with all of the insensitivities and annotations of others, not walking in your devastated shoes, would be the half mixed-quicksand, that our loved one's value, or our upholding of, is now foundationally, being constructed upon. Keep in mind the only certainty here, is that *your* loved one is immensely valuable, *TO YOU*; thus depicted, by the multi-million dollar structure. It does not mean everybody else will see or assess their worth, importance, significance, irreplaceability, and overall value, the same as you. That is very important that you accept that. That will later, play an active role during your quest for your new normal, in selecting who you find comfort in, or surround this new version of yourself, with.

Remembering above, there are many affects and disturbances that you will encounter, during this quest, over which you will have no control. Allow me to share with you some of my experiences with 'outsiders'. In this scenario, they do not realize how propitious it is to be deemed an 'outsider' in this story. I wish that I could trade places with one of the 'outsiders,' while never having an aspiration of them treading life now, in my shoes.

Every time 'outsiders' speak, during my journey of this pain-infested mission, my 'PTSD- riddled' heartbroken mind, re-writes the meaning of the words they utter. For example, I accompanied a friend for a routine EKG. The Doctor walked in and asked my friend, if they were ready for their EKG test. My mind whispered:
"I am experiencing an E-K-G of my own. Can you help me too Doc? Mine, is not an outpatient hospital medical test, as I am sure there is no device that can begin to gauge or monitor the actions of my wood-chippered heart. My EKG, is E-lbows and K-nees G-one''.

These are the words I uttered to myself, as I sit here, trying to show support, for a normal friend in a normal setting, after My Chelsea died. There is NO normal.

PTSD, is what this is, at its best. It will be covered in an upcoming chapter. This type, of incalculability, of people around me, and what I, myself am suffering, while alongside their normal moments, is just one example of the differences of the grief-born emotional abnormality and traumatized perspective that separate us. That same nefariousness of grief, separates me and the world, at every given moment, since August 7th, all around me even without their knowing it.

Infinitely ranging interpretations, such as this, are mentally documented daily with both genuine and non-genuine people, passing through my newly 'shattered' immeasurably transformed world. Even intended comfort seems to be contrasting in its effects, during my quest. Some people claim they are sad for me, but every single time they open their mouth, I am saddened to a whole new degree. I have to share these after-math verbal atrocities with you, so that you can either relate, or if you have said similar statements, you can now know how they made that heartbroken party you were speaking to, feel. Sometimes, expressions of sympathy are not empathetic or sympathetic at all, they are simply, pathetic.

I've had individuals tell me after losing my firstborn, that I *'should thank my lucky stars that I have at least 2 more children'*. Do you want, to know what occurs for me, when that statement is made?

Immediately upon hearing this, I feel like I am starring in some type, of twisted smothering prank show. But instead, of Ashton Kutcher jumping out, tears do. I will never thank stars or anything else, that I have 2 *more* kids. If I have 2 *more,* that means I have 1 *less* than I had. 1 less than I carried, inside, of my body, for 9 months, then in every other fiber of my being for 21 years. A person I nurtured, cared for, provided for, loved, and lived for, was now gone. I don't want more or less of anything. I want the same. I want what I had. I won't ever find comfort, in more or less. I will only find comfort in the same.

Have you ever said this, to someone, having lost a child? Despite your intent, that was one of the most hurtful, frequently stated things, I heard. Why would you think it is beneficial to me, for you to be making any statements, counting my children? My grief-born PTSD, makes me want, to push a magical button here. Not a button that brings my child back to this 'concentration-camp style cruel world', but a button that for a moment, reduces the number of *your* children, by one. I would then like to see if you think my daughter, is so disposable? Or that I would consider myself lucky, to now have 2 instead of 3 children? I would like to give you my shoes, if only for a second, and see if you can even fit them. My mind, in this moment, is now wondering, if I could, take away one of your children, not literally, but control your mind for a moment and have you feel what it is like to lose your firstborn, your first real love. After this exercise, I wonder, if your next statements, will be exactly the same with your child now magically gone. I already know that your answer here, is an unquestionable "NO". I bet before now, that never occurred to you, as hurtful. Did it? IT IS. And here is, why.

Each of my 3 children, held their own place in my heart. They are not interchangeable, exchangeable, replaceable, or compounded. The other 2, will never replace my missing one, nor, will they ever try that impossible 'un-do-able' task.

Now, since I do not possess that 'mind-controlling' button mentioned above, and since I *have* not been comforted but hurt further from your words, let me now explain, what will happen next.

Unbeknownst to you, your statement's effect has now prompted the awakening, of an unfamiliar version of myself that stands before you now, in the remainder of this and all future interactions. My 'Grief PTSD', which we will discuss, a little later in this book, will now take on the appearance of rudeness. Inauspicious, in my demeanor and tone going forward. I, now, will be depicted by you, as rude, as I have been called, so many times, since my daughter's death. I am not all of a sudden rude, **I AM HURTING**!

Any accounting, numbering, lining up, of my children, on your part, isn't consoling at all. I hope that you now understand that. The act of counting, re-reminding me, of my deduction, my loss, further causes impairment, to my already mind-bogglingly painful existence.

Now, with that acknowledgement, all future encounters with you, following this conversation, will not be with 'the forth coming or outgoing' me, at all. You will now deal with the 'guarded defensive' me.

My conversation with you will be minimal, if at all, because I have consequentially been made to feel I need an armored stance now. I shy away, due to your inability to discern what is appropriate to say to a person with an enormous internal fear that you will count my children again. Now do you see, what you have created, in me? You have caused my grief-stricken irrationality feature to conclude, you do not know what to say to the brittleness of a shattered grieving person. Now, in this book, my hope is that you *now* know, and are made aware of the significance of that 'standoffishness,' you witnessed, in myself or in others following your erroneous attempts to be consoling.

Now, did I solve that mystery, for you? Did I better define an explanation of what you have falsely labeled, as rudeness? Riddle solved. Since this is probably all new information, to you, this book has served its purpose.

The next hurtful 'comfort-labeled' message I was told was that 'I am fortunate to not have been left with a grandchild by my 21 year old deceased daughter, to raise'. Actually, it was said, "with so many young girls having babies at an early age, you are blessed, your 21 year old didn't leave you stuck, raising a kid". Really? Did my ears really just hear, what I thought I heard? By more than one person, on more than one occasion? Did you ever think that I would find comfort or be made to feel better, hearing that? Was your intention good? Do you know those above words stabbed me, as if the speaker was actually holding a beveled edge, newly sharpened, 48 inch ninja sword?

Now, allow me, to give you a window inside of the grieving mind.

I would take ANY PART OF HER, I could get!! If she had a 180 pound Rottweiler, when she died, I would carry it around in my purse, like a 5lb Yorkie just to be close to HER!! Now, how does that make you feel? Or better yet, how do you think your words made *me* feel? Better? My answer is an unambiguous, sound barrier-breaking "NO", yelled at the very top of my deflated lungs!!

These abovementioned statements cause added injury, to the already severely wounded. When I started walking off prematurely after being hurt, during your attempted consolation, I was labeled as a 'meanie'. Yet if you remember, even before my daughter passed, I was never a person that tolerated disrespect. So, in this new grief-PTSD state, I am so uncertain of what my retort will be to this brand of 'painful comfort,' that I remove myself abruptly, to avoid responding harshly to a person that actually had good intention. I quickly try to suppress the rage that comes with this pain in my response. That is the fragmented version of trying 'to think before I speak', yet only feeling the blinding pain, as your words just hurt the already devastated. Walking off, is all I can muster, due to what those words of yours just triggered. I have to consider their intentions may be from a non-malicious place. If that place in you, lack an ill will, you will need to acquire adequate understanding of this paramount devastation, to avoid actually being hurtful and ineffective in your consolation. For that reason, I am compelled, in spite, of my fragmented soul, to pen, this book.

Prior to my daughter's death, I was a strong-willed self-respecting straightforward individual that vocalized confidently; yet it was always safe, in that I possessed more than an intonation of 'thinking before speaking'. But this pain means that characteristic, can no longer be trusted. Just as none, of my prior automatic skills are reliable, this too prompts me to retreat, as oppose to responding to the hurtfulness. If that past version of myself, intermingled with the new fragmented shattered one, responds, to what now feels like a personal attack bursting with insensitivity and boasting of uninvited uncouthly opinionated rhetoric, there will be more than *my* feelings hurt, in this conversation. There will be terminations of relationships, as have occurred also, since the passing, of my daughter. My exiting a room here, is not rudeness, but it is all I can do to display my unwillingness, to waste any moments of my now shattered fragile life, with this person, that is oblivious to my crushed armor. I also start to feel they unaware of the effect, that they are having on 'this new' me. Presently, I only have pebbles of strength left, not an iota of extra to be consumable in ineffectual interactions that cause me further damage. I will need all of my wreckage, for a quest, for a 'new normal' for myself and those 2 children you reminded me, I only have left.

I even had someone, to approach me and say, "allow me to say everything I have to say, before you respond, Cat". Are you aware that *that* introduction just set off my 'be prepared to be disrespected,' button? Do you know how I know? Why, would you choose, an introduction of suppression, to a person that is already speechless with pain and suppressing every second, just to get through, the next second? If the uninviting look, on my face now, following that introduction, don't stop you from sharing that next hurtful collection of words, that you are prepared to spew to a woman that is hurt past her sanity, then brace yourself. Rather it be your personal opinion, of my daughter's manner of living or method of death, you have declared yourself adversarial with *that* introduction alone. If your true intent is comfort, you should never tell a grieving individual, when they can, or should speak during an interaction. My PTSD, to be discussed in later chapters, just queued up in my brain a translation: "Cat, here is my knife, don't scream or defend yourself, until I finish, stabbing you". Did you know, that is what, just transpired in my mind with that introduction?

During my quest for a new normal, I discovered that there are very simple instructions, to comforting a person like myself. Comfort, do not pretend to relate. It isn't relate-ability, unless you yourself have suffered the same loss as the person that you are speaking with. When I say the same, you have to ensure, not only that their manner of death is similar, but that the deceased's issues, while living, were the same, or that is not relate-ability.

What if the person you are speaking to and wanting to comfort, for instance, comes to you and says that they lost their kid in a car crash that involved a drunk driver? When you tried to comfort them, you immediately replied telling them, 'I know how you feel', followed by, sharing that your neighbor's cousin, lost her kid in a car crash involving a drunk driver, too. Did you just attempt to comfort them, saying 'I *KNOW* how you feel' and followed, with *that* story? Did you think *that* was comforting? Allow me, to educate you as we review the facts.

Did you lose sleep when your neighbor's cousin loss, occurred? Were you incapable of digesting food, after learning of that death? Did you cry so hard, that you actually lost your vision? When you heard the news, of your neighbor's cousin's child and every moment since then, did you lose *your* will to live? Did you entertain wanting to end your *own* life, when your neighbor's cousin's kid died? NO. You did not. That is not what *you* felt, AT ALL. So you are NOT feeling, AT ALL, what the person you are attempting to comfort *is* feeling. All that you just did, in your efforts, to minimize her pain, was told this devastated, crushed, suicidal mother, of a dead person you know. All that you have done is told her of another departed individual that made you feel ABSOLUTELY, NONE, OF WHAT SHE IS FEELINGS. You only shared your familiarity of a story which has infinitesimal similarities, of what her melted heart, was barely able to mouth to you, while she was seeking some relief, from her situation. Is that *now* clear to you, Can you *now* see that? You told a story. She is telling her life. Don't put your story up against her real life horror and sorrow. Does that make sense to you?

STOP TRYING TO RELATE! YOU CAN'T! That, is not comforting. That is quite insulting. If she was speaking with your neighbor's cousin it would be relatable, but since you are the story teller here, you are not comforting at all in these far reaching efforts to relate, regardless, whatsoever, of your intention. PERIOD.

Just to further convey the significance of the impact of this open-eyed nightmare, did you know that I couldn't even watch television for a couple of months following the passing of my daughter? Do you 'outsiders' have any idea why? Ask the truly grieving person you know. First, *nothing* was entertaining to me. 7 weeks into the 2014 football season of The Miami Dolphins, which I'd never missed watching a game since I was 5 years old, was when I finally realized that the football season had even started. I wasn't even clear of which day was Sunday, as I had no internal clock, whatsoever, remember? The real reason I could not watch television is there were too many triggers. During a quest for a 'new normal', you quickly learn that you do not have a bank of strength to draw from.

We, the grieving, have a 'zero' strength meter reading, and it is best to avoid any set-offs, set-ups, or breakdown enhancers. At any given moment, when a television was on, up would pop a story containing similarities, even in the most miniscule of manners, and a wipeout was most inevitably certain. It could be as simple as a pretty face on a commercial with just a shirt, similar to one she owned, and I would then be guaranteed a spot on the floor, afterwards. It is that simple. Something so trivial and insignificant to the regular mind, can give birth to a meltdown in the mind and heart of the truly mourning, sorrow-filled souls, like mine.

I only tell you of this, so that you will start to realize the severity and intensity, of the effect of a loss on the truly grieving. Also, to enlighten you that if a few seconds in a commercial can create such an emotional escalation, does that not speak volumes to just how fragile the truly grief-stricken, are? How cautious, do you think you should be, in the name of comfort, so as to not have adverse or detrimental effects? And so as to not cause further damage to the previously smashed spirit of this one you claim, to care for? If they, after losing a loved one they truly can't and won't live without, can't even watch television the same way? Does that one facet, give you any insight into this tumultuous journey?

This quest that we, the grieving, are now on requires that you relate or simply be there. That is it. Relate or be there. Provide comfort by saying the words, 'I AM HERE'. That is it. We will tell you what we need, or we won't, but at least no further damage will be done, by you, to a person that is already so severely damaged, that they now have to be, on a *Quest* to find *normalcy*. We are not, on a quest, for fame. We are not, on a quest for success, dreams, or even happiness. We are on an active battlefield, exhaustively, waging war for a quest for a 'new normal'.

Don't make our quest harder, knowingly or unknowingly. You are now empowered with an outlook or vantage point. Utilize that in locating your own 'new normal', in conjunction with your desire, to support the person that has suffered *this* loss. Thanks, to this book, you are now 'in the know' of how challenging a QUEST FOR A 'NEW NORMAL' can be.

3. NEW NORMAL
FOR FRIENDS AND FAMILY

Family and friends, if you are not the one that suffered the loss firsthand, you need to be educated in engineering a 'new normal' of your own. I am sure that you have gained some knowledge in the last chapters. A 'new normal' will be required of you going forward, after their loss, in order to relate, communicate, and most importantly not further damage the person that is most impacted by this loss at hand, while they themselves are on their own quest.

This, is by no means, a minimization of the impact or hurt that you yourself, experienced with this loss. You too, deserve condolences, but this is geared more to adapting to the person that is *most affected* by this loss.

For Example, you may be the uncle and deserve sympathy, for losing your niece, but your grief, will never equate to your sister's. She has lost her very own, child. No more 'tomorrows' with her *own* child! Do you get that? This is not the time for a power struggle, as that is how it will come across in your attempts of consolation, if you are not cautious. Even though you share a loss, be extremely careful here of your proclamations of 'relate-ability', as we discussed in the last chapter. You *can* damage your relationship with your sister, for example, or this grieving person, by expressing combatively, that your pain equates.

If your sister, keeps having, to 'out-grief' you or proclaim *her* changed life, just to be heard or comforted by you, she will start to withdraw from you. Be careful, at this time, to not allow the only interjections, outbursts, or even contributions by you, are that you are representing the significance of *your* memories or feelings and the validity of such. Your timed delivery is what will keep your sister, or the grieving, from starting to retreat from your brand of comfort. If you are erroneous in your delivery, distancing in your relationship will most certainly start to occur. This gap will mean you are losing the potential and opportunities you have, to actually help her. Be mindful of these methods, if comforting and consolation is truly your main goal.

Now, is also not the time to interject negatively, about your niece in the above example, regardless of your inside information. You can express all of your 'judgmentally-themed' statements to *your own* friends or network, but not to the closely grieving. It is also imperative, that you not express these same statements, to *shared* allies, as those individuals may share your statements, *to* the closely grieving. This will result in the same added damage as if, delivered by you, but being caused, actually, by *way* of you. Expressing 'judgmental' knowledge to the grieving, serves no beneficial purpose and will not lessen their mourning.

Any of the above, will be the foundation, of you quickly being labeled an 'outsider' and cause you to be avoided. Simply with the grievous one's PTSD rationalization methodology, you will be avoided, due to a lack of understanding being shown to her position. In the example of your sister, her loss, has created, an even greater protection field or duty to her child. Judgment on your or anyone's part, will certainly, be met with combat by this hurting protector. So here, balancing, not battling your grieving relevance, over hers, is the very definition of your quest for *your* 'new normal', as you, priority-wise, fall behind and second to your sister's grief and needs.

Some of you, family and friends, have the best of intentions. Unfortunately, you are often erroneous in your most solace efforts, despite your intentions. Simply put, this loss does not have the same impact and magnitude to you, that it does for the person, most times, that you are trying to comfort. You deserve condolences and sympathy, as you have lost too. But your sister, the mother of this deceased, has carried this child, *inside*, of her body, and gave life to a child, that will, no longer be in any of her 'tomorrows'. That fact, doesn't minimize or negate your loss. But your sister's loss is maximized in comparison. You will need, to learn to deal with her accordingly. You are trying to provide comfort and assistance, to someone that is generally too distraught, to convey the ineptitude of your consolation. Regrettably, I gathered research firsthand, after the loss of my daughter.

For example, I was told by a brother, of mine, after the loss, of my firstborn, statements like I previously mentioned. I couldn't believe that

MY brother, HER uncle, could utter the words, 'at least you have 2 *more* children', and 'thank your lucky stars you have 2 *other* kids, to live for'. Are you kidding me? I should not, could not, would not, thank any stars, or anything else, that I have 2 *MORE* kids. If I have 2 *MORE*, that means I have 1 *LESS,* than I had. When it was said to me by my own brother, it was far more hurtful, than when said by a supposed friend. And considering he is an insider, endeavoring for validity of his loss, as this was his niece, he should have known better. He should have empowered himself, with the obvious, of just how devastated I was, before he opened his mouth, causing irredeemable damage.

My brother's uttering, of the above statement, was received as a proclamation to my shredded soul that his hurt would never, ever, get near the threshold of my pain and loss. That ignorance on his part, resulted in immediate distancing, on my part. Further deemed negative uninvited interjections, of his, made all next interactions, adversarial, until I cut him out of my life, entirely.

Also, no truly grieving person wants to hear, anything that puts their missing loved one in the wrong or labeled in a bad lighting. That will pose no comfort and will get you ousted, from the circle of people, from which they seek consolation. It will never be known, if you could have helped in the future, because when it was most needed, it got presented poorly. The devastation of the grieving one can not see this supposed comfort if it is gift-wrapped in judgment and condemnation. Further consolation from a hurtful presenter will most certainly be rejected. Just as with my brother, I even started to resent him. Unlike the 'good intention-having' friend hurting me unknowingly, that was not the case with my sibling. How could my brother have been a good uncle and arrived at any of these conclusions, counting my children, and thinking that would be comforting? Or deem this appropriate to say, to me, this close to the passing of my firstborn child? I even stopped seeing him, as a good parent, for his own children. But there is so much more to that story. I will simply stop there, only drawing and recounting that basic fact to share with you. But that does bring to mind that you do have to consider your history before the loss, as well, that will play a factor as to if your comfort will even be received, after the loss.

Anyway, a good parent would never pass judgment on a grieving parent. Even if the parent is appearing to be fixating only, on their deceased child, a good parent could relate and would know, that when there is one missing, that *one* is the only child of the parent's focus. Initially, anyway, or until that kid is found, touched, hugged, kissed, seen, or safe. Being that you *know* that the other 2 children, in my case, are alive and well, is exactly why it appears all of my focus is and will be, on the lost or missing child, for a substantial period of time. 'Outsiders' need to be aware of that. For a parent, they will experience the above, regardless of the manner of their child's death. Death is death. Losing a child is losing a child. 'Outsiders' do not need to be preoccupied or equipped with anything other than that.

Also, if you are consoling, a mother like myself, after the death, of my child, NONE of your conversations, following a loss of that caliber, should contain numbers. Any audits, of the remaining amount, of my children, will assuredly create additional wounding. For my brother, to allow those words to come out of his mouth, created an unbridgeable void between us. If I had mustered any air in my lungs, to even be standing before him, that statement alone just bankrupted any improvement his comfort, could have conceivably, brought, to my devastated world. He is no longer a part of my life. I am better for it.

((There is so much to this backstory. It includes past abuse that had been suffered, at the hands, of my very own family, while my daughter was living. Now, there was no way I was going to make room, for this, brand of hurt, after losing my child. If you want to see the horrid events, containing my family, before and after the death, of my daughter, that grossly contributed, to her demise, read SAFE by D.D.T. Gray. It is a gritty, raw, expose'. It can be found at www.createspace.com/4969825 or on Amazon)).

Now do you see, how despite intentions, it is very important that you learn, how to console your loved one before you incite the heavily grieving relative, to sever all ties?

It was such a ghastly experience, after the loss of my daughter, that even, in the absence of motivation *or* strength, I still had to put this body of work together. I was affixed to changing the outcome, for others in my same position. I wished no one else to experience the atrocious aftermath, I myself, experienced. The loss itself was great enough, paramount. But additionally, to be on the receiving end of immense hurts, *after* my daughter passed? For the people that I know cared about me, I discern that their injuring me in this devastated emotional state, was unintentional. That didn't make it hurt any less though.

It is for those unknowing ones also, that I pen this book.

I feel that with assistance, after gaining insight, you will be able to equip yourselves with effective tools of comfort. It seems most people categorically, while having the best of intentions, still fall short in understanding, when attempting to console the residue of a person having suffered a loss of a great magnitude.

Yes, residue. Fragments, wreckage, rubbles, shards of the person you knew prior, is all that remains. Maybe your attempts of consoling the grievous one is falling short because you are trying, to comfort the person *you knew, before* the loss. Without being in the exact same position they are currently in, you are incapacitated in a sense. That is why I am imparting you with this information. The loss of a closely related loved one can cause such a massive amount of hurt that it takes so much out of them, that there is not much left of the person you *knew*, at all. You will need to proceed accordingly. You will find yourself constantly evolving, to remain effective, in the facilitation of this grieving person, you care about. Your desire to do this accurately, will be *your* quest for *your* 'new normal'.

One of the first things I said to all those that were concerned about me after the loss of my firstborn, is that it hurt so momentously that I wanted to change my name. I wanted to change my name!! Because I was *that* sure, that Cat Gray had died with her Chelsea on 8-7-14. Do you get the implication of grave (no pun intended) effect that I am expressing above, that losing her had on me? That this new resemblance, of me, needed to be renamed? I went so far, as to shave my head, change my incoming hair color, wear colored contacts and even, when writing my first novel, I did change my name, to D.D.T. Gray.

Because, the Cat Gray, the prior me, in all of my past outlooks and perspectives were no longer in existence after August 7, 2014.

Now that I have expressed how I personally felt, or how unlike myself I felt, does that let you know how much the person, standing, in front of you, sometimes after a loss, is not the same person that *was* present, before the loss? They are not, one in the same. And that genuine people, with that acknowledgement, is exactly why, you will have to find a 'new normal' in order to talk, help, or even remain, in the life of this 'new' relative or 'new' friend.

Let that marinate.

There are so many things I could tell you, to do differently, but the implementation and the continued efforts, will require *your* dedication and diligence. It will not be easy. But if you step outside, of yourself, for a moment and realize that the person, you want to comfort most, has had their life altered forever. Your quest, for a 'new normal', in relation to theirs, is only temporary though. If you devote sincerity and earnestness at *this* time to your quest for *your* 'new normal', for them, you will only benefit this person that is hurting beyond their existence and sanity. You will *not ever walk* in their shoes. *You don't have to*, in order to assist them, in their efforts *just to stand* in the ones they have been *forced* to wear.

Don't take simple interactions for granted. Every single time that you have an opportunity to speak with this grieving person, you have a pivotal choice and role. An option of taking that time and making it good or bad, helpful or harmful, uplifting or detrimental. That is just a fact. There is never a time that the grieving have the luxury, of forgetting their grief, so don't base your interaction, on rather they are smiling or crying. View each and every interaction as an opportunity, to improve, their anguish and sorrow.

I know, in my personal situation, I even wished people would stop being so normal, in their greetings to me even, after my loss. If they knew they only had 2 minutes to talk to me, why lead with "How are you?" The answer is, and always will be, HURTING! So think outside, of the box. Lead with statements like "it is good to see you" or "is there anything that I can do for you". The latter of the statements, do not ignite my 'turtle reaction' I call it. You know how the turtle has his neck out, but the second you do something remotely diminutive in his direction, he snatches his head into his shell? That is how the statement, by a hurried individual 'how are you' makes me feel. Don't be so regular. My life isn't regular anymore. The person, in front of you, is the farthermost from regularity as is humanly possible. Besides, if you lead with the later statements, as opposed to 'how are you', I can take it from there. But if you ask me how I am, you give me no room, to wiggle, from under my space shuttle, of pain, especially, if you are expecting a hurried answer. So don't be regular, it appears as insensitive to me.

Also, do not pretend to be a journalist and ask details of the manner or method of death, if it is not volunteered. This will not translate as comforting at all. In fact, that by asking, if it isn't volunteered, you simply quantum leap that person back, to the most painful single moment of their lives. And for what? To satisfy some overwhelming need, *to know*? It can't be for the benefit of the person, you are claiming, to be trying, to comfort. Rather you know it or not, they never ever leave that moment behind, except, for the briefest of sessions, when they are *actually* comforted.

Do not have your interaction themed or tainted with being responsible for dropping the grieving right back off, at the very moment, of their life, when their lives forever changed. The single moment, that they wish they could change, in all the moments of their entire lives the most, is the one you want to use your time asking questions about? They dream about changing it, they pray about changing it, they would use magic or trade places, to change that single moment. And now you will use your opportunity, to take them straight there, that is the destination you selected here?? Think about that.

For me personally, I chronicled this paramount of mine in 122 page book called <u>SAFE by D.D.T. Gray</u>, that I told close friends and those genuinely concerned for me about, after the death of my Chelsea. I didn't do this, to become an author, and gain fame. I did this, to not combust, from the pain I felt and that others made me feel afterwards, also.

Combustion or suicide was inevitable for me, after losing my Firstborn. In this state of devastation, along with what I was made to feel afterwards, it left me to conclude that no one understood. So to stand before me asking for details, just seems disrespectful even. I just feel that if you didn't care enough, for me or her, to have read what would be a conjoined 122 page suicide letter. Fast forward to now, thinking you deserve an answer, now? I gave you the story that she would have told from beyond the grave, combined with the story I told *instead of* going to my *own* grave.

All the genuinely grieving people feel this way. If you want to be in their world or comfort them, stop taking them backwards to ground zero. That is not going to produce good results. The only time *that* moment of the initial loss, should be the theme of the conversation, is when THEY MAKE IT THE THEME, not YOU. You stand here, in the face of an active PTSD terminal chronic victim and use the air in your full lungs, to say 'why' and 'how' and take the devastated to that very moment of devastation?

For me, I found so many things wrong, with that statement. Besides, what I said earlier, there is also the fact that I sit here, incapable of taking anything but shallow breaths, right before your very eyes. I can't even inhale deep enough, to fully inflate my own lungs or heart, yet you are blinded, oblivious to that fact. It comes across as a lack, of genuine concern. Any quest for a new normal, for anyone that loves me, should know that you were given a window, into my devastation, in fact, a passenger seat, in this overwhelming ride of mine, from start to finish, in that book. My writing it, was because I was **not** going to be able, **to say** most of those things. My ability to write those things, was for your benefit, as well. I was giving you all the answers, so you would know, how to co-exist, with me, this new me, not the old me, accordingly, from that second on August 7, 2014, forward. I also was seeking justice for my child in all the rage-filled pages as I didn't know how or if I would even go on in life.

My introversion and not divulging those things, in our following conversations, was my exasperated way, of sparing you from the post traumatic life, I am wishing you knew something about. And I guess I thought if I wrote it all down, I would be spared of EVER being asked about what happened. I know now that is unrealistic. But in your quest for your new normal, you would have realized I felt I had no other choice.

So do not become a journalist, to the devastated grieving ones, only make statements, after you have done your homework, or simply, from your heart, and let them take it, from there.

Most times, the details, of the loss are the hardest, to accept and swallow and transition past, for this most grievous person. In my personal experience, I volunteered all that I could volunteer, in my gut-wrenching first novel. Writing, was my saving grace. It kept me, from ending my own life, to ease the pain, of my loss. As well as, the painful things discussed, in this book that occurred, by genuine and unauthentic both, after the greatest loss known to man. My family even made me feel I had to retreat, for survival. I even went into hiding for 14 days after putting pen and paper. Feeling like an alien, in and to, the rest, of the world. So anyone asking me, personally, how and why, is just rude, because I gave you a 122 page answer, from beyond my own grave. I even have to re-read it, at times, as I was just a shell, of a human, in motion. That is how stripping, this pain is. Your interview afterwards, is not beneficial to me, which will end your benefit of being in my world, as I have nothing left to engineer juggling added hurt or appeasing forgery and calling it, friendship.

As you have learned, there are so many moving parts, of grief, for someone that is truly inconsolable. I am sure that you were aware of this, but potentially, not to this degree. It is imperative, if your intent is to ease any portion of this journey for the survivor you care for, you will need to ruminate how, to incorporate, this itinerant element.

Be aware that time is not, in the same increments, for them, as it is, for you. Never make statements about their state of grief or monitoring progress based on your schedule. Grief is not linear. If you witness them during a time close to the actual loss, and see those same painful eyes months later, they may have some measure of composure. Most times this composite of composure, has been created from recoiling most 'outsider's' reactions, into giving the appearance, of improvement. All of the things we previously discussed, including inappropriate consolation and comfort tend to only aggravate not ease the impending grief. It is never over, for them. It is never graduated from. So try your level best not, to interact, with inclusions of time markers. No leading statements of conversation, should contain anniversary markers, such as 'it has been a year or more so I know you are better'. In my case, just a couple of months, after my devastating loss, a friend said 'I'm glad to see you going on, with your life'. I abruptly walked away. I will never, nor could I, would I, should I, ever get over the loss of my child. She will always be a part of me and my everyday life, good and bad.

Also, in an effort to comfort, please refrain from imparting your personal indications of time awareness. I assure you, the grieving has no clock, of sorts. Sorrow does not come with an ending time for this magnitude of pain. That is still true even, when they return, to some resemblance, of what their lives were prior, from this enormousness life-changing, life-altering, loss.

Remember, when you do not know what to say, you probably should not say any more than the following 3 words: I AM HERE. Allow the person suffering the loss the hardest, *to lead, drive*, cry, not lead at all, not drive at all, and just allow them to be. Afford them the comfort, of being the one, controlling the interaction, the tone, the context. After all, did you say that you wanted to *be there, for **them***? If you are there, *for THEM*, you will be there, *for them, how they need you to be* there. Do this with no pre-conceived notions or actions, of any caliber, that originates in YOU. Do you get that???? If comforting is your true intent, you will open your mind, as you read all of this.

The reason your presence, in their world will constantly transition is because the person you are comforting, is metamorphosing so frequently, due to having no bearings, of their own, as you saw in earlier chapters.

This newly unstable person, will be 'roller-coaster-ring' daily, sometimes hourly, as they have yet still to experience a whole cast of 'firsts', that will most definitely, set their progress back. Just as the title of this book, there will be a 'First Christmas', a 'First Thanksgiving', a 'First birthday', that 'first phone call' where their beloved is asked for, 'that first appointment', where they are asked how many kids they have' and not even that is the culmination, of the major triggers, alone. They have to take that 'first family photo', that 'first car ride pass the scene', that 'first trip to the beach', and so many more milestones, on this already tumultuous rocky road.

Those constant indicators, that reminds, and re-reminds them, of their loss, will make their quest, for a new normal, ongoing and ever-changing. Your continuance, in their world, will mean your new normal, will have to be, of the utmost, fluidity.

4. MEN HURT TOO

From a man's perspective, research has shown that 'male grief' is quite uniquely complicated. Men are innately designed to protect those they care about. A loss of a loved one, sometimes give them the impression, of a miscarriage of their security. They also process grief inversely, being that they are not accustomed to displaying their emotions as well, frequent, or as open as women. The vantage point, of the grief-stricken male that you care for, needs to be dealt with in an individualized manner.

First, their genetic build of fortification makes them experience a sense of powerlessness, in the face, of accidental or untimely death. Whether they are a Grandfather, Father, Son, Brother, or Husband, their grief has a large element of guilt entwined, when they lose someone they love. They have a tendency, to feel that they should have or could have changed the outcome. It is their innate initial response. The reason that all 'outsiders,' near this inconsolable male, needs this knowledge is, to provide you with assistance, in formulating the correct message of consolation. Being aware of these facts, should prompt you to convey components, specifically addressing their inability, to have impacted the outcome. Lack of control, is far different, from failure. You need to encompass this dissimilarity, in your efforts to impact the gravity of the masculine complicated grief phase, to be most effective.

After losing my 21 year old daughter, I had to be preemptive in assuring the clarity in this distinction for my 20 year old son. Their closeness in age, coupled with him having been the only male in our home for most years of their young life. I quickly realized this had to be my first priority. If I had any chance of providing any solace to my shattered son. With all, of my bearings lost and all previously automatic functions rendered incapacitated, I had to figure out a way to provide consolation, even, after my own devastation of losing my Firstborn. I realized this task couldn't be a choice, it simply had to be done. You all that have suffered loss, please take this into consideration immediately for the males involved.

My son and his heart was far too important for me, to not attempt, to minimize, his inconsolable distress even before my own. That daunting task is why I felt the need, to share this part with you. To empower you, in this priority, with understanding of what it entailed.

The message here seems almost simplistic. The reason this step often gets skipped is due to the fact that there will be, most times limited, if any, outpouring on behalf of males. They, just as my son, still will attempt to undertake the role of the protector and display strength for me and his younger sister. The reason I dedicate this chapter, to my Son, Tre, is that he, needs to know, that, is no longer the precedence of duties, he should assume. He has lost the person that was by his side, closely at his side, his entire life.

All parties reading this chapter, have you done that, for the males in your world? If you lost a child, did you insure that their brother knew he is not powerless, he just lacked control of this particular conclusion? If there is a father, grandfather or husband that this applies to, have you relieved him of the self-perpetrated rollercoaster, that he will certainly continue to ride if this disparity is not recognized and disconnected from?

The other prevalent fact in 'masculine-based grief', is that their fortified predisposition is to refrain from frequent, or any, emotional outbursts. Society has inaccurately imparted most of the male persuasion with the misconception, that emotional outbursts or simply crying, is an insignia of weakness. That simply is not true. Stating it is not true, is not effective. The manner, in which you inculcate it, in your acts of comfort, *can be*. First, it takes you acknowledging that fact. That is why, from the depths, of my complicated grief, I heaved myself to comfort my son, as well as, to write these words to you.

My personal experience with this, was another of those problematical next steps, for which I was not equipped, at that time. The love of my son, impelled my hurried edification in this matter.

The depth of agony, in my loss, of my best friend, My Chelsea, rendered me incapacitated, in countless aggregates of ways. The unexpected passing of my child, was not a life event I could have ever been prepared for. Yet the massive weight still could not be an obstruction of my motherly duties. After all, my loss *was* his loss. If it was unbearable for the leader of his family, namely me, I had to step outside of myself and decipher a facilitation, for the crushing anguish he was most assuredly, combatting.

Whenever I could get some hyperventilation-free seconds, all that I wanted to do was walk up to my son, and breathe. Breathe as if to inflate his lungs, a conscious CPR of a person, whose eyes are wide open. If eyes are the window to the soul, in his, I could see the door to his soul, slamming shut, from the pain. He didn't want air from me, he wanted a reversal of our reality. After all, he had always looked to me to fix things, in his life. I later realized his inability to look at me, this time, meant somehow he knew I wouldn't be able, to fix this for him, for us. I couldn't even stand up. I couldn't meet him on any eye level, as the floor, closets, behind the bed is where I kept finding myself.

First, it is most important, to keep or start any dialogue with a grieving male, I learned. Keeping in mind, if you are awaiting signs of emotional distress, those may never be visible. The realization that this loss has occurred, on their watch, or during their lifetime even, can be paralyzing. The male isn't just dealing with the outside elements, of this loss, there is a whole battlefield of a waging war, internally.

The powerlessness, I spoke of earlier, was fast at work with my son, and I could blatantly see that. He kept putting space between us, even though he remained near, at the same address, he often times was not in my viewing range. I would often come upon or locate him, when I could muster the strength to stand up, and I'd find him in an emotionally distraught state. I myself, being in disbelief, just seeing him this way would often cause me to break down further and he would maneuver his placement once again, *away* from me. This cycle of 'hide and go cry', continued until I could identify this is what was occurring.

Even in my 'zombie' state, I knew I had to find a way, not an *'our'* way, just find *a* way, *for him*. I couldn't let him continue to feel this massive life-changing grief, showing all over his face. For him, I simply had to. That was the only thing I was certain of. Even though, this time, my 'mind over matter' self-philosophical approaches, were all malfunctioning and wrecked. How could I help him? I just kept telling myself, I can't lose him too. Even if robotic, I have to define a course of action. I *needed* to help him. I needed help to help. My mind went to my niece, Tavia. She had been like a daughter, of mine, her entire life; more than a sister, to him and Our Chelsea. She was just as devastated as he. Yet I knew my first step had to be, finding him something or someone to hold onto, as he kept going away from me. I couldn't allow him to be alone with his male misconceptions that he could have, or should have, saved her. I was as vocal as I could be to him, to remove these misconceptions for him, hoarse voice and all. I was clear to him, every single chance I got to be in front of him. Reiterating to him, that he could not have saved his sister, even though, I was not yet clear, myself, that I could not have rescued her somehow. I simply vocalized, trying to move this mountain from him.

But this very moment can't be spent on anything that I am feeling. I am numb anyway at this point, so back to him, my focus *must* remain. Since his innate battles, common of males during loss, are fast working and internally overwhelming, I must get someone he can relate to, at least temporarily. My niece was the answer here. I got her with us and kept her there, for weeks. Now his 'hide and go cry' episodes will, at least, contain a shoulder, as devastated as her shoulder was, he didn't have to feel he had to suppress, with her, as he'd felt with me.

This is an important fact for you to take note of, if you are reading this book. Even before you know how to help your male that is drowning, find anyone that they are comfortable with, to offset their 'alone-time'. As their unaided time will not be spent productively or even rationally. They will isolate while processing this desolation, but often times, only equipped with the misconceptions we spoke of above, that are certainly a part of their genetic makeup simply being born a man, but not to their benefit at this time.

Cycles such as the above mentioned are detrimental to males.

When I could get some seconds of reality-grasping clarity, I realized my son and I were in the middle of a tug-of-war, in our universe. An unnatural battle of loss of our identities. Who we were, as people, as a family, had just been transformed, eternally. It was most definitely an identity crisis we were suffering due to grief. We had lost 'our girl' and the world's axis had shifted and disassembled our existence, as we knew it. When loss of someone that important, to the both of us occurred, we could not be who we were, just as I spoke of earlier, not even to each other.

It is pivotal that you understand this. You will not get the same male that you had, before the loss. Your attempts, to comfort the man you _knew_ will be ineffectual. If you do not embrace that the masculine persona, in front of you is someone you never met before, you will be ineffective. You have to prepare for that. I, as the mother of 3 children, including one humorous comedic-genius of a son, had witnessed the death of both of us, in one single act of losing her, all right before my very eyes. I was fighting to get any composure, so I could be his mother, while at the same time, he was suppressing all of the floodgates he was experiencing, so that he could be my strong son. He wanted to provide strength for me, as he had done so many times, before that dreadful day. I wanted to be his rock, like I had done so many times, but now I was a pile of gravel. No rocks in sight.

I have to tell you my personal experience back and forth, to let you know how I arrived at a space, that you can find a valuable message within. A message that you can inculcate and implement, in your personal situation, with your grieving male, as well.

After getting someone for him to relate to, I knew I still had to keep pushing on _for_ him and _to_ him. I had to check-in, with my baby boy, my Prince, at least, until I could inflate one of my lungs ¼ of the way. Even breathing was no longer automatic, as you could see, in the first chapter of this book. Again, the reason I chronicle this for you, is with hopes of giving you the very assistance I needed, that I had to configure, on my own, notwithstanding the fact, of being in my most bewildered distraught state, of my 43 years of existence. All that considered, I still _had to_ pilot this crashing plane, alone and with my son aboard.

You learn on any airline's flight, in the event of a crash, you are supposed to put your oxygen mask on first, before helping the person next to you. When you are a mother, I assure you it is exactly the opposite. If we were on a plane, I'd hold what little breath I already had, and secure the oxygen mask of my child first, even while risking my own life to do so. That is a real mother's reflex, a real father's reflex, a real parent's reflex. (I was a real mother, Tre didn't have a real father, he was a deadbeat) Anyway, when it came to saving MY SON, It is nothing that you think about or anything that a stewardess or even God, could tell me to do differently. God could not tell me to not save Tre first, after losing Chelsea, because all I could clearly see is that I could not, would and should not, lose him too. I couldn't even pray about it. Not due to a deficiency in my beliefs or in the Higher Power, but due to my respect for God. I couldn't talk to God, because all that came out of my mouth, in this agony, was riddled with cussing and was immensely rage-filled. At that moment, this moment, this day, this hour, I was the mother of a lifeless child and I was angry at the world. I was angry, at all parties involved and the prior bullying that got us here. (If you want the backstory, on the responsible parties that cost me a child, you can find the raw gritty expose' SAFE by D.D.T. Gray at www.createspace.com/4969825 for the uncut graphic version).

I couldn't even allow the complex manner of my loss, of my daughter, to obstruct my vantage point now, of my son's preservation. She would want me to save him. I had to find a way to keep moving, not forward, not progressing, not empowered, and *just* moving.

This is something that we all that have suffered a loss have to remember. We get so visionless, in the relentlessness of the pain that we ourselves are undergoing, that we are extracted and distracted from the benefiting, or even functioning of those around us. I couldn't stay that way now, this is MY SON. It would be majestic, if we could pause our pain after a loss, to indemnify the welfare of those that rely on us, in my case, my son. We would love to completely absolve ourselves, of any and all responsibilities, including caring for anyone else's needs, but this is just not the way. It is imperative that you know, saving your male has to consist of your involvement, even may have to be under your leadership, despite your craters of desire.

This daunting task won't be easy. It wasn't easy for me. It will be one of the most challenging things you will ever do, following the most difficult time of your life possible. It will be the most problematic because you are not yourself. Grief has a way of robbing and stripping the skills and techniques, you have previously utilized, in the maneuvering the maze of life. Just as I expressed to you before, there is an identity crisis that accompanies complicated grief. Now with that in mind, do not be alarmed that you have not and are not equipped, prior to now, to save the men you care about with their processing of this same loss. It is the very *reason I share my struggle with you*. I need you to clearly see, that sometimes the pivotal steps needed, to save a man after a loss, *won't wait* for our strength or desire, to return. It needs to happen, *in spite of* our feelings, because time is of the essence.

The importance of time here can't be expressed enough. The longer you leave your male consumed and absorbed, with that type of pain, the damage can be irreparable. Hopefully, you have already learned here of their complications with grief and the processing of their suffering. You have to implement further action, but now with awareness now, going forward. That awareness needs to be all encompassing, of their unique outlooks, in the face of their loss.

Now that we have identified the grief's identity crisis, the comfort-power struggle, and the misconceptions of men, while grieving, as it occurred for me and my son, we can't stop there. I couldn't stop there. I had to take his overwhelming need to display strength and guide it. He was strong. He always was, and he always will be. He just couldn't display an acquiescence that his power was not the missing element that got us here; that led, to our loss. That only meant my work, offsetting this misconception of his, had to rise to the top of my strength-less being, despite the loss of all of my bearings. I couldn't allow him, to further misconstrue his role and compound his pain, in front of my very swollen eyes. He is my leading man, I will keep striving to service my pulse, my son, systolic to the diastolic pressure of my heart, silenced, in losing Chelsea.

Next, with all of the above acknowledged, my realization became that I can't sanction him to stay in this timeless space that I, myself am stuck in. At first, that was all I wanted. Him with me, everyone else gone, just me and him. After observing all of the above, including his suppression of his painful inner turmoil, to appear to still be my protector, I realized that was not the way. That would have been the way, to parent my son, in any other loss, but not this one. Our identities were lost, remember. I kept having, to remind myself, of that. Therefore, forcing our togetherness was like trapping strangers, on the most hurtful day of their lives, in a closet. We were that 'so' unlike ourselves, even to each other.

I needed, now knowing what I know, to give him activities, to give him 'time-fillers', with hopes they would absorb some of his grief. Not chores or tasks that required he pretend to be in a satisfactory emotional state. Not events designed to distract him, as my goal is not, to facilitate his internalization or spiraling into an unspoken depression. I needed to encourage activities for him, revolving around his sister. After all, she is the very person that was overwhelmingly occupying, both of our minds, hearts, and souls. I myself, was already absent, of an internal clock or any time-keeping mechanisms. Sleep was an uninvited stranger, food was an antagonist and anything that organically happened, to tell me how many minutes, hours, days, or weeks, it had been, since losing my 'Chelt,' was officially nonoperational.

I didn't know if his experience was the same, but I did not want to discuss that with him, anything damaging or make him focus, on the non-functioning parts of himself. I just needed to plug something in his psyche, along with the pain, he was experiencing. I told him I needed him in charge of selecting and designing the line of t-shirts, that celebrates her life. I next told him, I needed him to personally start selecting music playlists, for any life celebration events. Music had been all of our best friends, separately, apart, and together. I knew that by pushing him, off the diving board, into the pool of music, he would find comfort, in their songs and the memories that music would incite, in his brain and heart. They had loved music and dancing, I had the videos and memories to prove it. But now, I even had a glimpse of hope, by walking into a room and hearing him laughing, even moments after crying, and if only for a second, during his newly assigned task of 'Music Man'.

I map this out for you, to educate you in a conquest, I had to mêlée through on my own. I was never clear of the progression, the tentative next steps, I was only clear on the impetus, MY SON!

You cannot await the recommencing of your strength, desire, or energy to match. You cannot even wait for your devastation to ease. I assure you, I still lack strength. My devastation is still, at an all-time high. But my progress, even in writing this to you, is designed to comfort my son, through the paramount of our pain, even to this day and to never allow Our Chelsea, to be forgotten.

I have not checked out, on my son's wellbeing or checked it off of my to-do list, as if it is completed, simply because his tears have lessened.

Due to my heightened self-taught awareness of the male grieving process, and the significant role my daughter played, in my son's life, I would have to build up his emotional improvement on that same love. There will be no internal battling, as is common for men, if the focus of our continued family, contains her, just as it did, before we lost her in the conventional sense.

He, Angela and I have band forces and started a Movement, The KCA Movement, The Keep Chelsea Alive Movement, where she is holding her place, in our family 4-pack, and solidly in our hearts and mind. You will read about The KCA Movement in the last chapter of this book. She, is now the priority of our daily functions, as we champion to keep her beauty and purpose alive, in this world, and to make a difference in her name. Her brother is now the General of that campaign. We are even touching lives of people she did not even know. Her brother, now has a little more strength. That is all due to him gaining momentum, through the abovementioned steps and now musically. He has ignited his creativity, and together we, me, him, and Angela remain functional, by starting and driving a Cause, that orbits the very one that we loved so much that we refuse to live without her. You will learn about The KCA Movement, in the last chapter of this book. If you want to cheat, you can go to www.thekcamovement.com and read all about it.

Keeping my male, my son's grieving in front of my own, I had to stay openly aware to his moods and state of mind, even still, to this day. The character, I created to write my first novel SAFE, D.D.T. Gray was extremely rage-filled, just as my son's musical character General of his squad, too, had rage inside during this grievous time for us. I didn't suppress or try to stifle this expression or anger of his, in regards, to the loss of his sister, in fact I encouraged it. I allowed him to be angry, if he was angry and never actively tried to change or divert these feelings of his, as they presented themselves. I created an open environment to keep allowing the outpouring of this misguided strengthened part, until he could channel it, on his own, to correlate with the loving brother he was. If there was disappointment in his inability to save his sister, he was allowed to express that, without judgment and always, with an invited ear from me. It was painful to hear at times, but my son and his wellbeing was the focus, of these actions. You will need to do the same.

It is most important, that you do not suppress or try to shackle your male's feelings with yours. It is important that they be allowed, to process at their own pace, fluctuating, as they see fit. All the while, supported by you and given time fillers, until they can fill their own time with grief absorbers. By allowing them to live through and live out their grief, as they are comfortable, allows them to progress and not internalize. My son is now writing music, of his own to honor his sister, where he can cuss about his sister or express any other feelings that he is feeling, that are unique to him, as a man dealing with his loss.

The lesson here, is to not allow your concern for them, to overshadow what they are *actually* feeling, at that moment. Encourage them to express THEMSELVES, not what you think they should or should not be feeling, at this juncture, of the quest they themselves are on. That freedom is important. That encouragement of that freedom of expression, regularly, is important. That is how you comfort your male, as your grief and their processing of grief, is different, even when the person you are grieving over, is the same.

Your love of that male, will require that you continuously 'check in' with them, always providing an open platform of judgment-free expression. Encourage them to feel *whatever* it is that they are feeling, for as long as they choose to feel it. It is *THEIR* grief. Just stay aware of just how much Men Hurt Too.

5. GRIEF PTSD IS REAL

PTSD. When you hear those letters, what is it that you think of? Soldiers, right? They are a large source, statistically, for the development and credentialing of this condition. Rightfully worthy, of having their trauma defined and recognized, as they truly are the bravest of the bravest. Yet, they are not exclusively the owners of this wide-ranging, mind-bogglingly, sometimes paralyzing disorder, anymore. The untimely Death of a loved one, can and has been proven to cause PTSD.

Indicators of PTSD, include 'rollercoasters' of irrepressible emotions, ranging from despair to rage and often cycling occurs, in momentary spans, with no provocation necessary. A single event so horrendous, that it forever, singlehandedly, changes a life, and not in a good way. This changed deficiency in stabilized moods, created by the velocity of having experienced this occurrence's magnitude, occurring after a trauma, are definitive of this disorder. This fluctuation in emotions, resulting even in physical stress and pain, in the body and mind, often make it hard for victims of PTSD to function day to day around mentally and emotionally healthy people.

The loss and circumstances of the loss of our loved ones, determines the range, volume, and presence of Grief-PTSD. Of course losing a loved one is never without grief. PTSD isn't grief. Grief is grief. PTSD is epitomized, in loss such as unexpected loss of a child, by a parent. This inorganic occurrence most definitely creates a trauma. This trauma makes Post-normality, almost always non-existent. Post Trauma behavior associated with the loss of a child, has to be relearned or contrived efficiently, just to have the appearance of post functioning, absent of flourishing, just functional, in the eyes of all those surrounding this new PTSD Victim.

What symptoms of Grief-PTSD, have you experienced?

_____

_____

_____

_____

_____

_____

_____

_____

_____

_____

_____

Like a devastated mother that I met in a support group, that lost 2 children within a 5 year period to Suicide, she is most definitely the poster child for PTSD. Nicki Narcise Gregg found her 21 year old son, 'Joey-boy', her best friend, J. Joseph Gregg III, hanging, days before Christmas in 2003. She is actually the one that cut the rope and tried to save him that day, to no avail. Do you not think that the trauma of her loss, and how it occurred, enrolled her in the PTSD membership plan, for life? As if that was not bad enough, 5 1/2 years later, Nicki loses her Kristina Marie Gregg, her 32 year old daughter, to Suicide also. Krissy left behind 4 children ranging in age of 3-12, just as 'Joey-boy' left behind a 5 year old Son. Nicki's inability to stop grieving, or stabilize her emotions, typical of this understandable onset of PTSD, has cost her volumes. She has experienced isolation from many friends and family members due to her PTSD.

My personal experience with PTSD, following my Daughter Chelsea's unexpected death, made me want to share with the world, not just the perspective through my eyes, but to formulate a bridge of our vantage points, so as to assist others that are impacted by this type, of onset of PTSD.

My daughter was my best friend. She was 21, and we lived 15 miles apart and spoke on the phone 6 times a day, most days. Her being taken, from me, on any given Thursday, August 7, 2014 to be exact, and all that followed, including never getting to say goodbye to her, My Firstborn, created the trauma that my newly born PTSD, is based on. If you want to know that complete story and the raw expose' following, that ineradicably put me in the PTSD club, pick up my novel SAFE by D.D.T. GRAY, at www.createspace.com/4969825 , which will put you in the VIP seating area of the origin of my PTSD, up front and center, with those 122 pages.

My first signs of PTSD, was my inability, to receive any comfort, or feel any consolation, from anyone. Everything that was said to me should have been said another way, per my shattered heart. My recognized PTSD, meant I was now a patient, and without the proper awareness, by the speaking party, this and any other interaction, was most certainly going to exacerbate my internal tsunami. First, as seen in the initial chapter of this book, there is an exacerbation that occurs every morning, when it is Grief-PTSD derived from a loss. I generally have 5 seconds of normal, a few blinks of my eyes, then I 'RE-REMEMBER' the death of my Firstborn. That 5 seconds, being the only happy awakening at the greeting of my day, which quickly gets stamped out when the PTSD clocks in, after that initial 5 seconds. Every decision and mental manipulation, after that 5 seconds of PTSD-free peace, is an effort, a strenuous effort, where there used to be, no effort required.

What were *your* very first signs of Grief-PTSD? (Even if you just now realized that is your condition)

_____

_____

_____

_____

_____

_____

_____

_____

_____

_____

_____

_____

_____

_____

_____

_____

I use to be self-motivated, focused, driven, ambitious, and even a business owner, that could 'out multi-task' any experienced corporate driven individual. I use to be a speed reader that specialized in analytical accounting reports. I could assess and find common denominators in errors or likeness and formulate solutions, from a simple mental snapshot of a full page at one time. I was a solutions specialist for a range of businesses, as I was a meticulous problem solver and could always increase corporation's profit margins, from my contributions alone. I had a career accolade, once, of collecting $12 million dollars in 45 days. I built a widely recognized name, for myself, for more than 2 decades in the medical financial administration world. I've helped start-up companies and established corporations alike, and they all sang praises of my abilities to accomplish the impossible. Before the loss of my child and the onset of my Grief-PTSD, that is.

Of what skills/skillset, do you feel, Grief-PTSD robbed you?

_____
_____
_____
_____
_____
_____
_____
_____
_____
_____
_____
_____
_____
_____
_____
_____
_____
_____
_____
_____

How has that effected your life, in light, of that now missing skill/skillset?

_____
_____
_____
_____
_____
_____
_____

To give you a microscopic glimpse of insight, here is a fictitious, yet insightful author, talking about me: 'text message from PTSD' it reads:

"THAT woman, just described above, that you all KNEW, actually DIED August 7, 2014, when her daughter died. So listen up World, what you see, is NOT what you get. Who you KNEW, is not who stands before you, now. She looks similar. You will even try to deal and relate to her, as you always have. You will be mistaken. You will be misunderstood, because she is walking around feeling misunderstood ever since she lost HER baby. You may even be scolded and exposed, to the appearance of hostility in her. She isn't hostile, SHE IS HURTING! You never knew of the anger and rage she had inside. It is because she never knew a pain like this. That is all. She is still a beautiful specimen. Here is a tip for you- FORGET EVERYTHING YOU KNEW ABOUT HER, just listen to her, now. If she speaks. IF she does not speak, just sit with her. If she does not show up, don't judge her. Her Ruler, which she measures all things by, she finds it in 100 pieces, on the floor, by her bed, every single morning. The sad part is, she will spend all day today, like she has every day, since her Daughter's death, gluing her ruler back together. Yet when she falls asleep and wakes again, it will, without fail, be on the floor, next to her, in 100 pieces again!! Tomorrow, will repeat, day after that, will repeat again". (End of text) *Signed, Cat Gray's PTSD.*

If you could write your text message, to the world, from your Grief-PTSD, what would it say?

_____
_____
_____
_____
_____
_____
_____
_____
_____
_____
_____
_____
_____
_____
_____
_____
_____
_____
_____
_____
_____

_____
_____
_____
_____
_____Signed_____PTSD

PTSD becomes Post Torrential Sadness (after) Death, in this case. Same letters, same effects, just additional meanings, in additional patient types of this now devastating debilitating Disorder. Does that text message above, make you understand anything different or more about the survivors of loss, that you previously encountered? Or that Mother, like myself, having outlived one of her children? After you write your version above, buy and gift as many people as you choose to, with your version, included in their copy of this book. They will be empowered with your vantage point. Do you know how powerful that is? Do the work. Start to make those that you care for, understand your Grief-PTSD. Trust me, they want the answers. Answers that only you can provide. Only you can take them inside of the Grief-PTSD, now happening inside of you. You may also want to give a copy, of this book to anyone that you know is hurting or has been devastated, by a loss of a loved one and encourage them, to do their work, by writing their story here, as well. There will be more participation by you requested in the following parts of this book. Don't skip ahead. It is important that you stop and actually write your answers, so that you will have those in mind as we go forward. Trust me, please. Let's go on.

PTSD, wrapped in grief, creates the appearance of an 'auto-pilot' effect. Do not confuse auto-pilot with cruise control. It is not a propulsion, of stabilized forward movement. It is an appearance, of auto-pilot, in the sense that there is movement. There is also a vehicle of sorts. It looks the same on the outside, but for all intents and purposes, please know, absolutely nothing, on the inside, of this hypothetical mode of transportation, is the same.

Imagine going to your car one morning, and there are no seats, when you open the car door? There is a wheel, but the steering column is missing? What do you do? What about when the gear shift has been ripped out, and no mechanisms are present for smooth, forward, expected propulsion? There is definitely cosmetic features missing also. No preprogrammed radio stations, no constant working lights, just coming on and off as they can, I suppose. That my friends, is what the auto-pilot vehicle, driven by grief is like. A POST traumatic vehicle, only resembles the fully functionally equipped method of transportation, it was, the morning before the loss of a loved one. The loss of a child, in my case. This vehicle looks like others, from the outside, but on any given day, there is no destination it is guaranteed to reach. After all, there is no steering column. There is no working horn, so at any given moment, there can be a crash, without warning, to any and all bystanders. Does that frighten you? Can you imagine being me? Or the truly 'Grief-PTSD- possessing' heartbroken individual, unwillingly, finding ourselves strapped into that car, behind the wheel? It isn't a vehicle that anyone would intentionally select or sign up for, but it is the only type of mobility available to the grieving.

Who are the people, in your world, that you feel have been effected the most by your non-working horn (per analogy above) that have been present for crashes?

_____

_____

_____

_____

_____

_____

_____

_____

_____

_____

Describe a crash(per analogy above):

_____

_____

_____

_____

_____

_____

_____

_____

_____

_____

_____

_____

_____

Describe an intended destination, but upon being strapped in the Grief-PTSD vehicle above, you did not make it?

_____

_____

_____

_____

_____

_____

_____

_____

_____

_____

Now with the awareness of Grief-PTSD, in someone you care for, there are elements that you, as an 'outsider' of this PTSD, need an explanation for. Have you noticed how the truly grieving, even after a substantial amount of time appear to be Bi-polar? Besides the internal loss of bearings, previously discussed, do you know that you are a contributing factor? You, the family, the friend, the mate, of the PTSD-carrier are often, to blame? How so, you may ask? I will tell you.

PTSD from grief is painful in every imaginable way. This type of pain, produces banks of sadness and inundations of tears. These uninvited feelings are barely controllable, by the carrier, if at all. But when most PTSD victims live in their truth and allow their actions to mirror their emotional state, 'outsiders' are often uncomfortable. Your discomfort is often made apparent in your reactions and responses. Your 'curtailing style' actions, as well the judgment-themed comments, we discussed earlier, generally by you, the non-PTSD carrier, is often a source that makes the wounded, U-turn, at a moment's notice, either for your comfort or to declare that you desist. Read that again, if you need to, but that, in and of itself, is a direct stimulus, to this knee-jerk reaction, mislabeled as 'bi-polarity'.

What has 'outsiders' done, to you, to make you 'U-turn'; appearing bi-polar? (Be very specific. This will also serve as a reference point for identifying triggers, at a later date.)

_____

_____

_____
_____
_____
_____
_____
_____
_____
_____
_____
_____
_____
_____
_____
_____
_____
_____
_____
_____
_____
_____
_____
_____
_____
_____

'Outsiders', hopefully, by reading this book, you are gaining insight, into the instability created by grief-PTSD. If you are deemed an 'outsider' here, in this book, consider yourself lucky. So let's continue. Expectantly, this information will produce alterations in your future actions, in regards, to the grieving survivor. If your heightened awareness can encompass this newly shared knowledge, of the impact this loss is having on the survivor, hopefully you can start to design an appropriate course of action. It may require diligent effort, on your part, to reduce the judgmental overtone and unpalatable responses in your interactions with the anguished. This is your choice to work at it, if you truly care about this mournful soul in your world. By doing so, inevitably, you will reduce the turnabout-like transitioning and spiraling of the grieving. This will require work, which is why it was stated that you yourself would need to find your own 'new normal' going forward. Most of the appearance of being bi-polar and inconsistent in moods, by the grievous ones, can be attributed, to a broken individual having to recoil, based on your judgmental proclamations.

Have you 'outsiders,' ever told a grieving person, that they 'should be better' or 'over the hump' by now? Or that enough time has passed, that they should not be in the emotional state that they are currently in?

Brokenhearted ones, who said this to you? What exactly did they say?

_____

_____

_____

_____

_____

_____

_____

_____

_____

_____

_____

What are your top 3 unforgettable recounts of an 'outsider', using a time measurement, or unfavorable statement, against you?

1)_____

_____

_____

_____

_____

_____

2)_____

_____

_____

_____

_____

_____

3)_____

_____

_____

_____

_____

_____

Have you ever encroached upon a grieving person, with your time markers, showing disapproval in their deficiency of progress? Do you realize the impact of that? It is equivalent to you buying a billboard, over your house that flashes in neon lights, "YOU CAN NOT BE YOURSELF AROUND ME"! This person's life, is no longer normal. The Grief PTSD has stripped away all normalcy and rationality. They won't be cognitive that you did not mean to scar them or scare them into feeling that they have to be a certain way. Their vantage point tells them you demand, that they be less emotional, more like you, around you. It becomes a conveyance that your comfortableness is the priority here. Was that your intention? Regardless, that is exactly, what your time-marking disapproval creates in this uproarious tumultuous broken sorrow-filled mind of ours.

Now, the uninvited 'broken self', over which we have no control, has to do one of two things, to be in your life after our heartbreak. We have to either avoid you or be counterfeit around you. How much advancement, do you think you are contributing to our quest, by displaying your disapprobation, not repeatedly, but even once? Instead of comforting or improving our PTSD, you are now categorized as a trigger and a bestowment to our already vulnerary traumatic life. Were you aware of that? I hope that now, you can be made cognizant of your consequence on our PTSD-riddled journey to get better. Be an asset, not a liability to this cumbersome newfound role we have been heaved into.

If you are an 'outsider', what is it that you have said, to whom, that knowing what you now know, wish that you could take back?

_____
_____
_____
_____
_____
_____
_____
_____
_____
_____
_____
_____

Maybe you should gift them, with this copy of this book, with your insertion above, now that you have a better understanding, hopefully, after reading all that you have read thus far.

I need you, with all prior things considered, to realize that Grief PTSD is real. It is real hard. It is real painful. It is real difficult to function while possessing it. It is extremely imperative that the world knows that Grief PTSD IS REAL!!!!!!!!!!

6. S.O.S. (SAVE OUR SURVIVING-CHILDREN)

The loss of a loved one doesn't *just* change the lives of the grieving adults that are so devastated that they have, to attempt to acclimatize the remainder of their existence. There is another entire group distraught, by this earth-shattering loss that we have yet to discuss- THE CHILDREN.

The youth that survive, losing someone that had solidified a place in their hearts and lives, are most definitely impacted, extensively. There is, assuredly a cave left behind, in the soul of the children. The weight of death of someone they loved can be immensely crushing. It will require that we be instrumental, in re-defining their lives, in light of the absence of someone who would have otherwise played a key role in their development and future. Their little saddened hearts have experienced a pain that we, as grieving parents, would have traded our lives, to keep them from ever having known. But here we are.

In this book, we are intentionally *just now* getting to the beautiful sad children that are deeply affected by loss. It is not because they are at the bottom of the priorities on this grief-stricken journey. Essentially, it is due to them being the *most* important. We have to design a plan of action containing the establishment, implementation, and nurturing of their coping mechanisms. Strengthening these fragile young ones for their own quest, has to take precedence now. Despite all things previously discussed, your responsibility has to become strategizing for their wellbeing, or at least their ability to breathe. They will need us.

The earlier chapters purposefully walked you through the vantage point of the grieving adults in a very specific order for a reason. The surviving children are *the* reason.

This book chronicled the tribulations of a tumultuous journey, with hopes of a 'new normal', defined, as a constant moving destination. That certain 'mountain climbing insider information' was next shared, in this body of work with the supporting cast of the grieving adult, needing stabilization in their own 'new normal'. The focus was to provide insight to all of the adults involved first. To identify the alterations necessary to circumvent adding, to the massive undertaking, of the broken hearted adults after losing someone they love very much, as we will need all adults as well as they can be for this next feat, of THE CHILDREN. Next we paid special attention to the adult males that were most certainly hurting, uniquely. All the while, staying mindful of the commonalities of the truly desolate adult males and females alike; this book next sought to strap you into the voyage of Grief-PTSD. Collectively, you were empowered. Equipped with this insider's knowledge so that your understanding could lead to consolation and genuine comfort versus judgment and added injury.

Addressing all of the adult matters of grief, was not because they were the priority, but because *all*, of the adults, that come into contact, with the brokenhearted children, *will need to act with Knowledge*. No more, of the added hurt from the supposed 'good intention' place, while the outcome is adversarial to that intent. These children do not have the luxury of deciphering and deciding that your objective was good when the words you stated, hurt them further. This misalignment of actions is not acceptable. There can be no irresponsibility or ignorance tolerated, in regards to the inconsolable unhappy children. You will need to make sure that all adults, KNOW HOW, to be there for these young ones.

Their future depends on it. I *literally* believe we can reduce the numbers of SAD children. Did you know that it is the SAD children that end up with health issues and the type of depression that requires medicating? That same avoidable condition and medication can lead to all types of issues including their overall health and wellbeing, including body image issues (after being given steroids) and all types of insecurities in the children. ((WOW, I just 'got' what she meant about the 'Invisible Ones', mentioned in the first chapter of this book, Dear Diary. This had happened to her (taking of steroids) and taking anti-depressants, which created body image issues. She felt those issues made her ineligible for the 'cool kids' club. Wow, you the reader, just witnessed a breakthrough, for me, in real time. I JUST realized what she meant about 'Invisible Ones'.)) Anyway, these insecurities are sometimes the direct result of the fabric/quilt of their lives being changed, so drastically, after having someone ripped from their world that they can give birth to these issues as well. I think with education and insight, we can even reduce suicide numbers of the youth. The Youth that end up completing this act, due to being overtaken, by their grief.

You have to realize that even their quality of life can be compromised so devastatingly, in the absence of their mother, father, older sister or brother that they once looked up to, or whomever this person is that they lost. They cannot emotionally afford to be exposed to unawareness and insensitivities of the 'outsiders', on top of this type of injury and agony. The children lack anything in their reservoir of injured innocence for added wounding. They will not be able to endure, without an aggressive supervision of their consolation, by you. This will include, ensuring that all of the adult parties avoid, all of the previously discussed, erroneous attempts to comfort their fragmented spirits. Compounding pain, from all of the 'outsiders', atop of their anguish from this loss alone, can have irreversible adverse effects. We cannot allow this to happen.

If we, the grieving adults, have the previously discussed tsunamis inside of us, despite our decades of strength and experience, how much more will the inexpert unarmored children agonize? How long will they hurt and to what degree? You have no control over the first but you can lessen the painful impact and provide direction with the latter.

After the life changing loss of Our Chelsea, my oldest, there was my son, Tre, whom we discussed in the chapter 'Men Hurt Too'. Then there was my baby Princess, Angela. My 11 year old, beautiful, all-around, spirited 'Angie' as Chelsea called her. She was most assuredly devastated, after finding out her 'Sissy' was not going to be home, ANYMORE. I couldn't just take her anywhere that her sister was located, ANYMORE. There would be no more weekly sleepovers for her, no more texting funny pics, no more 'Sister's Day' that they enjoyed every other Saturday. Just all of sudden, NO MORE. I can even tell you, that, as I type this, I am having to do so, through flooded eyes. That hurt to Angie, was like another loss. Just as I'd been devastated, I had to be devastated again, with hurting for Tre, and devastated yet again, carrying that hurt for Angela. As a mom, that was my job.

I felt that pain triple-fold.

Literally.

I am now trying to breathe, to get through this for you all. You need to know this.

I can't even promise you this chapter will be as cohesive as I originally intended, as I just ran smackdab over a landmine of my own 'TRIGGERS', like we discussed earlier. When I had to think about Angie and her brain absorbing 'NO MORE', with her 'Sissy' she loved so so dearly. 'Meltdown Ville', it was. 'Wheeeewwwwwww', I'm trying to breathe ya'll.

There is a wealth of information that I have to share with you, but there is a reason, I am actually writing this chapter last, even though that is not the placement in this book when you read it. So please forgive me, if I ramble or seem to not be as structured. The information is what you need, understanding is what I need now, from you, to get through this.

'Angie' and her 'Sissy' were extremely close, as they lived only 15 minutes apart and whenever she wanted to go to her sister's house, I would readily take her, which often occurred twice a week, most weeks. Besides those impromptu sleepovers, there was always designated days that Chelsea dedicated the day to their sisterhood. Every other Saturday, Chelsea ('Sissy') spoiled her 'Angie' with trips, to the Taffy store, movies, beach, mall, salon, and whatever 'Angie' chose. Her 'Sissy' didn't enforce a bedtime or nutritious diet or anything else of structure, against the wishes and dreams of her 11 year old baby sister, during those visits. I am happy to know that Angie had that, sadly only for 11 years. It often reminded me, of what My sister Phyllis Pugh Myers, that I lost just a year earlier 9/3/13, had done for me, when I was 'Angie's' age. I had previously thought that was the hardest thing I'd live through, losing my sister that had never judged me. That loss was followed by the death of my father, just a month later. But I can say unequivocally, the death of my child made all of life prior hurts, all combined together, pale, in comparison.

So I couldn't fathom what 'her baby Angie' would think or how I would get her through this, initially. But just as you learned, in the 'Men Hurt Too' chapter, when it came to my son, I simply knew I had to do something. I knew I had to do *anything* to breathe life into her 11 year old heart.

First, the only fortunate thing I had at hand, was that she was out of town when it happened. She was spending some time with her dad and his family, who lives 256 miles away, as it was nearing end of the summer break. So fortunately, I had a moment. But just a moment, as I had to protect every aspect of this for her, I couldn't let my 11 year old find out, the same way my 20 year old had, ON FACEBOOK! (No, my 11 year old does not have a Facebook, but her family on her dad's side does). My 20 year old son, was the one that told me. Anyway, all of those painstaking seconds, moments, and hours are chronicled, in the book titled SAFE by D.D.T. Gray, mentioned earlier. I can't revisit those here. The start of the summer June 4th, had been Angela's graduation from elementary to middle school, and who do you think was in attendance and had made her day special? Her 'Sissy'. I had the pictures, videos and all mental seconds of recounting it, to prove it. Oh, My Dearest God, HOW? DEAR ANGIE?? Sissy Help Me!! I just had to figure something out. No idea of what, where, or how, just knew that I had to not let this mountain be thrust down on her 'Angie'. I couldn't.

You can see the state I was in, in earlier chapters. Once the WHY was identified this time, and 'her ANGIE' was the center of this 'Bulls-eye', I didn't have a choice but, to autopilot my nothingness to something, AGAIN. I knew My Chelt would want nothing more, than for me to save 'her Tre' & 'her Angie'.

I knew if I could just get her 11 year old heart through the initial news, the very thing that Tre needed, that I needed, would be what Angela needed. To keep Our Chelsea Alive! NO OTHER OPTION FOR US!! I had to introduce these things together. I had to hold her days through the crying. Yet controlling the interjections more, but the same principle applied, I had to let her have freedom to express how her heart interpreted her devastation. I held her. Phone off, TV off, world paused, and let her scream. I couldn't give her the same respect I'd given Tre, of following his lead. He was older.

I had to drive her. I had to guide her. I had to pilot this crashing plane. This plane that was about to crash again!! This time, with my 11 year old aboard. My statements every other 45 seconds was that 'You know, *SHE will never really LEAVE YOU!!'* That was alternated with, '*I KNOW IT HURTS, BABY'. I did* know how bad it hurts. I also knew, I would NOT want to stop her tears, here. I would just hold onto her as best as my strength-less arms could and let her kick and scream, while the floodgates of her soul opened. I wouldn't stop her. If there was no magic button I could push to reverse our reality, I'd have to *let* her cry and scream. I'd known this feeling. I hated having to stop crying every time I cried. I WANTED TO Cry!! I NEEDED to CRY!! I knew I wouldn't make that mistake, with Angie. I wouldn't try to stop or slow her crying, no matter how bad it felt as her body crumbled more than once from the weight. That may sound odd to you. But let me convey this simpler.

It is like having the world's biggest steam pot above the biggest fire known to man, known to this 11 year old now, and that lid being held on tight. WHAT TO DO WITH THAT TYPE OF STEAM? And INSIDE OF MY 11 YEAR OLD?? NO WAY!! No, I would get this top off, burns, lacerations, melting skin and all. I would simply hold onto her, taking in all of her hurt, on top of Tre's hurt, on top of my hurt. Even though the fragments of me, were once again fed through another shredder, I would hold onto to this top tightly, so that there would be no way possible, that that lid could lock that type of steam inside of My 11 year old, HER ANGIE!!! I could close my eyes, I didn't have to think at all, or have to have any strength for that one, which I assure you I had none. I could still just close my eyes, and my DNA would not let loose of the grip I had on this lid. I gave her my undivided attention for days, as if I could pause the world for her. I just know I couldn't let it land on top of her. As she would tire out, I would take her to a funny memory, and just as she would get that image, she would cry and alternate smiles for screams. I wouldn't break her cycling or send her running back inside of herself. I would catch the few smiles, and simply say YEP MOMMY GOT A PIC OF THAT TOO, AND WE WILL HAVE TO MAKE THE WORLDS LARGEST PHOTO ALBUM…and just never stopped her or drive her past *her* moments, *their* moments, now solely *her* moments to recount in a safe setting, invited and begged for, for *her* to elaborate on as she could, but respecting this was the introduction of *her* grief to mine, but still *hers and hers alone*. I hadn't lost My Phyllis, My Sissy when I was 11. I could help her, but I was powerless to take this walk for her, in her shoes as she loves her 'Sissy' and 'Bubba Tre' so deeply. I had to let her hold the wheel of the rollercoaster. But only WHILE SITTING IN MY LAP.

Keep in mind, this was her initial days only with this grief. She would have the appearance of driving, I'd give her that. Why? Simply put, it was to avoid branding her with introversion or suppression for the remainder of our lifelong journey. My letting her cry and scream, no matter how those razorblades of her cries were slicing me, I had to endure it. Whatever I did initially would stamp her course of action for the remainder of her quest for her new normal. I would love to tell you that you have to be strong for this type of torture and suffering. But as for strength, there was none. You cannot, absolutely cannot, wait for the return or rebuilding of strength to occur. They, the sorrow-filled children, do not have that type of time. You just have to keep the reason 'why' and the 'who' in your scope. I would re-adjust and re-align as many times as needed during this tear flooding task of letting my 11 year old convulse from pain, in my arms. This is of utmost importance.

Remember, in earlier reading, you learned that you either had to avoid or be counterfeit, based on the actions of the person comforting you? THAT WAS MOST IMPORTANT HERE!! I'd already made that mistake initially with my 20 year old son. I'd wanted to fold up and crumble in his arms so many times, but after identifying our power struggle of both of us wanting to be the strong one for each other, I'd drove him to mourning away from me. Remember? But do you also remember, at the start of this chapter, I said there can be no trial and error when it comes to the babies? Don't think I told you that, because I read it somewhere. I told you that, because I lived it! I couldn't be so broken that I couldn't handle her breaking, convulsing and all. I couldn't be so broken that she would want to help me, by stifling her screams and cries, even though I needed all the help I could get, I'd have to just take it in. I had already made that mistake with my son. No room for error with her. I couldn't let her, get a pebble worth, in her psyche, that she couldn't be HERSELF, with me!!

I couldn't ever let her feel she would have to pretend with me! I'm sure I'd drove my son to that. Here, I apologize to him, in front of the world, from the bottom of my tattered heart. I would have to make this right for him with how I handled her. She could scream, cry, laugh, sing, scream some more, I just needed that impression of freedom, to be made apparent here.

The very thing that I'd longed for since standing in front of that cannon on August 7, 2014. And I can tell you now, that that was the single most important function of those horrific heartbreaking days. I didn't have to keep telling myself anything, My DNA was going to do this, for 'HER ANGIE'!!

How did you tell the surviving children? What was their response??

_____
_____
_____
_____
_____
_____
_____
_____
_____
_____
_____
_____
_____
_____
_____
_____
_____
_____
_____
_____
_____
_____
_____
_____
_____

And did you think comforting the children, meant stopping their tears only? Or what was your definition, of comforting the children?

_____
_____
_____
_____
_____
_____
_____
_____
_____

The other thing that was of utmost importance to me, was to unify the adults on the very things that I shared with you earlier. I instructed all adults in her pathway, to contact me or reach out to me if there were any questions, comments or concerns on her behalf. I took aggressive control of this facet. I was not going to let Angela endure or even encounter things that I had been subjected to as well as the questions and issues my son had dealt with. THAT WAS NOT AN OPTION! So I had a conversation with her father, all relatives and adults that she would come in contact with, in my absence to let them know of their accountability and definite role in Angela's newly uninvited unwanted post-'Sissy'-life. I would do this, every time she slept. That needed to happen simultaneously immediately and just as importantly as all protection I could possible give her, in this battlefield of devastation.

I was fortunate, in one aspect with Angela, her paternal side, of the family also had her best interest, at heart. Even though one of the casualties, after Chelsea passed, was the closeness Angela's father & I had shared in our years of co-parenting. After I lost Chelsea, he wanted Angela front and center immediately for my caretaking, memorial services and such. I didn't agree. I couldn't even breathe. I had no voice, as I had screamed myself voiceless. I needed a little time, he and I didn't agree. Our civility came unglued. We have yet to resume a steadied communicative existence. Now we just each parent Angela from our own corner. After successfully co-parenting Angela together for 11 years, Angela would still be ok, even if he and I were not constantly having dialogue. She wasn't aware that we had come apart, we provided a united front for her. Besides, her paternal grandparents, Martha and Curtis Lee Barnes, loved my baby girl and could relate to where I now sat.

They had lost their 21 year old Angela, just as I'd lost my 21 year old Chelsea. In fact, my Angela was their Angela's namesake. My Angela's dad had insisted, on remembering his sister, at the birth of his female child; thus our Angela, had been named after their Angela. I had never known the impact, of their loss, until I talked to Mrs. Martha Barnes, after My Chelsea got her wings. I couldn't even say much, but she was one, of the few people, that said everything right. I quickly surmised, Mrs. Martha was perfectly comforting because she had had front row seats to this pain in her very own life. Now I could only take from that, which I didn't tell her, that I hope I'd helped her somehow, remembering her baby girl Angela in the naming my baby after hers. Never even knowing the value that would now play, in my heart. I couldn't even thank Mrs. Barnes properly, as the English language seem to be tear-filled jargon, I only hoped she would recall that I'd honored her Angela, with my Angela.

I had originally picked to name her Morgan Cadence Barnes, until one night Angela's dad, woke in the middle of the night and said he wanted her name to be Angela, after his sister, that he lost in a car crash, that he loved and missed very much. I didn't bat an eye, I simply quickly said "Sure". I now know *that* pain in his eyes, is now Tre's pain. One day, Tre will ask his girl to name their daughter after his sister, Chelsea. I didn't hesitate, when I was asked, thus our Angela. And one day when Tre ask his girl, to honor his sister, I hope *that* female doesn't even pause, after all, The Universe owes me that, Karma too.

Now decades later, I quickly deduced Mrs. Barnes was in my same pain still, even decades later. I wanted to lay my head in her lap and then we alternate, but I lacked the strength to travel to her. I inhaled and exhaled normally, knowing she would be pivotal in the supervision of caring for Angela's new shattered heart, when on the Barnes watch. I'd love her for that always. That part was easy. We had always loved each other.

I would still have so much work to do with all the other 'outsiders' that Angela would come in contact with. Let me paint this for you in the simplest terms possible. If Angela's heart was a portrait, priceless art work, it was now in 1,000 pieces. I had to build a special frame, in which to put all the pieces. I couldn't make the priceless picture whole again, that would take a lifetime, but at least by securing her perimeter, I was protecting all, of the many many pieces by safeguarding it, with this framework. I'd build it strong. Not because I had the strength but because I would buffer all that could reach any one of those 1,000 pieces. That, I could most definitely expect to keep on the top of my 'to-do' list. I would not fail to address, face, fight, cuss, or defend this framed fractured masterpiece. That was not an option.

You will need to do the same. You will build this hypothetical frame. What is the purpose, of the framework discussed above? It is an encasing around the fragility of the brokenhearted child. It is surrounding them with safety measures. The cell phone was a tool, to be discussed shortly. I would never be out of reach for her, during her quest for her 'new normal'. She would never have, to weigh added hurt, if so, it would only be the seconds it takes, to dial my number. Talking to the adults, in her path earlier on, was further added measures of reinforcement in the building materials of this frame. After all, just as with you, keep in mind, this frame contains one of my three most valued possessions. Strength or voice or not, framework sooner than later, meant safekeeping, even if I couldn't speak.

How did you handle the people that were, in immediate contact, with the surviving child/children?

_____
_____
_____
_____
_____
_____
_____
_____
_____
_____
_____
_____
_____
_____
_____
_____
_____

If, you had not built your framework prior to reading this, or lacked the strength before now, what will you do now?

_____
_____
_____
_____
_____
_____
_____
_____
_____
_____
_____
_____
_____

It is never too late. Even if added damage has been done, to the child/children, up to this point. Change it today. Have a dinner, a family BBQ, write a letter and make copies, anything to reach the nearby adult individuals. Add reinforcement, to the framework, surrounding the child/children. It is not too late. When you know different, do different. It is that simple.

Remember, they are our prized possession, enclose all of the pieces left. You will eventually be able to recreate your masterpiece, which is them, but only, to the degree that you have preserved the pieces. Understand?

Now with the task of constructing or re-constructing the children's framework, comes the heartbreaking necessity of gathering the pieces.

In gathering the pieces, the other fact I had to keep atop my cognitive existence, was 'her Angie's' innocence. I could not resort, to any of those statements of consolation used by the masses. I personally had found no comfort in those statements, even when the person's intention was of an upward nature. Initially, the goodhearted tried to ease my pain with things like 'She is now in a better place', 'God knows what he is doing', 'God called her home' and the like. Later when the blindness of pain subsided a tiny bit, I later knew all of that was true. But here, now, before my 11 year olds bloodshot eyes I didn't want to express any such things. Her innocence, the compilation of how her mind works, fixed with knowledge of how deeply she loved her 'Sissy', meant those phrases could not be uttered at this time. Why? When talking to a person that still thinks SpongeBob could be mayor, if I attribute the end of her 'Sister Days' to God, She may blame HIM, whenever she is missing Her. I had to stay cognitive, that her belief system is my belief system, but giftwrapped in innocence and simplicity. My belief system tells me God selected to receive my child, after her painful journey here, on earth, ended. But I had to arrive at that. I couldn't see anything but my pain, initially.

It is important you to stay aware of that, as you do not want to give the children further issues that they have to make sense of or mentally struggle with at this time. I was not going, to give Angela anything that would require that she calibrate it. Calibration, in an 11 year old brokenhearted mind? Do you understand why I didn't want her belief system, consisting, of her innocently thinking SpongeBob should be mayor, to paradoxically conceiving God took her sister away? Those minds are one in the same. That is the very definition, of innocence. To believe all is good, until there is bad. Her virtuousness is not to have to rationalize that there is bad, such as her new agony, and that one in the same is good for her 'Sissy', which is God calling her home. Do you understand that? I could not connect the two extremities of those two things together, for this beautiful devastated child. I don't want her to have to decipher or reconcile *anything*, in this now shattered world of hers. I am living one second at a time, but my motherly instinct has to think years ahead for her. I don't know how, but that is, what had to, and did, happen. You will need to do the same.

Did you or others say some of the above statements to the children? And have you provided an updated explanation, to disconnect any mental turmoil this may have created?

_____
_____
_____
_____
_____
_____
_____
_____
_____
_____
_____
_____
_____
_____
_____
_____
_____
_____
_____

Just as we have learned, on more than one occasion, in this book, that grief is not linear. I knew I could not be inside, of Angela's mind each and every time something would trigger a memory of her sister, as they spent a lot of time alone minus me. What I did know, that I did have control over, was my being there for her.

We went phone shopping days later. I made sure she had in hand, a phone that had SKYPE loaded on it. This is one, of those things I would urge you to do. Days and weeks later, I convinced her that this was like having 'Mommy', in her pocket. That made her smile. She would never need me and not be able to reach me, from this day forward that was of utmost importance. Also after a loss of this magnitude, the surviving child/children become somewhat paranoid. They develop fear that they will lose everyone and anyone they care about. I knew the phone would make her accessible to Tre and myself with the touch of a button. Besides, that newfound paranoia, which is common to powerless children after grief, I also had to keep in mind all of the times, discussed earlier, of when someone randomly said something, that wiped you out or turned you inward. We are adults. I could not allow my child, my Angela, her 'Angie' back, into the world, without being able to reach me, at a seconds notice, and the SKYPE allowed me, to look into her eyes and her into mine in the event of any wipeouts, meltdowns, flashbacks or Just because. Remember, I am now on full alert to guard my framed pieces of 'her Angie'.

During one of the lighter times, Angela suggested that we go see a movie, as I feel her internal clock was unknowingly resorting to 'Sister Day'. I chose to oblige her, even though I was quite leery, as she and I had not been to the movies without her 'Sissy', it would generally be the 3 of us, or the 2 of them. I had to go anyway, shakiness and all, as I had to follow her lead on her energy level. The movie she selected was Disney's 'Big Hero 6'. As we were leaving her father's house, he said to me, she wants to show you that movie because of the funny line the main character keeps saying 'Fa-La-La-La-La'. True, my children were all quite silly and playful, but I knew she hadn't returned to the silliness. So there had to be another reason that she was so insistent about *this* movie. Just as I accompanied my friend to the EKG, and what I experienced and what she experienced was polar opposites, I knew Angela was selecting this movie for a different reason, other than the comedic reason her father thought, I would just have to see. She may have seen the jovialness the first time she saw it, as her 'Sissy' was still alive then, as far as she knew. So why was she now adamant about me taking her broken-spirited framework to this particular movie?? I had to find out.

I have no idea how Disney marketed this movie, as I had never heard of it, maybe it was during the time I could not even watch television. But knowing Angela had seen it before her sister passed and now was requesting to see it again. I had to get to the bottom of this.

Allow me to interrupt myself, and tell you that if there is a child in your home that is age 13 and younger, dealing with the loss of a loved one, you have to take them to see Disney's Big Hero 6, or purchase them a copy of *that* movie. I am getting excited just trying to tell you this part.

Angela's dad, just like my friend at the EKG, was right by my side but had no idea what was going on in the mind and heart of the brokenhearted right next to them. I'd have to prematurely conclude Angela saw something he did not.

Angela selected this movie, or Chelsea did, knowing that Angela would get the value of the main characters being in her same situation. The main character *loses his sibling in death* in the movie. His sibling dies! The main character goes through the cycles of grief, being enraged, being enormously sad, crying, fighting, and screaming, and all demonstrations of wanting his brother back, after the loss. When that part came up, in the movie, Angela squeezed my hand, as the tears streamed down her face. I simply held onto her tight. My stomach was an origami knotted collection, as Angela squeezed my hand tighter. I was able to see what she saw that her very own Dad couldn't equate that this was the reason for her re-selecting this movie. I'm not done, but what I will say here, is if you have not been having open dialogue, with the surviving child/children, this is the way to open it back up, guaranteed. There is more.

Remember me telling you all earlier that I realized our, meaning, mine, Tre's, and Angela's 'new normal' *had to* contain keeping Chelsea Alive. There was no other option for them, or for me. I knew they would need that. Thus I started The KCA (**K**eep **C**helsea **A**live) Movement. It was my way of ensuring that even though we did not have Chelsea in the conventional sense, she would never be out of our lives, not even for a day. We could still see her, we just had to find the *new* way. We could still have her with us, we just had to have her with us in a new way. This Disney movie, Big Hero 6 goes on to do just that! The main character, once he leaves the rage behind, is given ways, even from beyond the grave by his beloved, on how to see his departed brother this new way!! You have to see this movie!! By the time it was over, Angela had the biggest smile on her tear-clad face. That smile also confirmed that she had heard everything that I'd said all days prior, that her sister was never leaving us and would never be out of our lives. This movie just added a video to those conversations, now. It is as if Chelsea, used her wings to fly down write, produce, direct and star in this movie. I won't tell you anymore than I already have, topped off with the urgency of your needing to show this to the sad child/children and be prepared to do your work immediately following. Wow, I am still amazed at that film, which I felt was heaven sent, by her 'Sissy', no doubt. It was so effective, coupled with my repeated efforts showing her how we would look and see her beloved sister now, that her bloodshot eyes were now widened and looking for signs of her 'Sissy'. It worked immediately!! The Spirit of Angela was now so temporarily consoled, that when she walked out, she ran up to the large AMC sign and said and I quote:

"Mommy, take my picture, (as she positioned herself, in a 'hugging' pose, embracing the bottom, of the 'C' of the large AMC sign). I said "Ok, baby", she continued with "Mommy, AMC means **A**ngela **M**ommy & **C**helsea, SEE, SHE IS RIGHT HERE WITH US ALWAYS (as she hugged The C), JUST LIKE YOU SAID!! GIRLS DAY AT THE MOVIES, Angela Mommy and CHELSEA, JUST LIKE ALWAYS!!"

I snapped the photo, as my heart skipped a beat!! I will cherish that photo and that night forever, I knew then her "Sissy" was not going, to let this mountain, crush her "Angie"!! The tears came streaming, but they were tears of joy.

I hope that at this point, you are feeling empowered by this book. My First Christmas was set in motion, outlined, inspired, and demanded by the same 'Sissy' that picked *that* movie for her 'Angie', and now for your surviving child/children!

She is a phenomenal woman, as you can see by now. Remember, this is HER gift to the world. Do you feel gifted? I do.

She will always be one, first of the 3 greatest gifts I ever received. The KCA Movement, had to be created! The world will benefit from keeping Chelsea ALIVE!! Our world of course, as well!! Don't worry, if you have not started your movement yet, your KCA for your 'Angie', the next 2 chapters will show you how. The KCA Movement, join it!! Be sure to hit 'Like' on our Facebook page, The KCA Movement, and also go to www.thekcamovement.com , especially now that you know the power of the woman behind it!!

I hope that you have experienced a breakthrough, during this read, but maintenance will still be required with these innocent brokenhearted babies. There are other things that you can do as the things Angela and I did and still do. I located every picture of them together, and printed them, as most were digital, in my phone, on her Facebook, others Facebook pages, each and every one of them that existed with the 2 of them framed together. Angela and I took an afternoon and went and purchased all supplies to make a scrapbook. I bought her index cards and told her over time, as she would feel like it, (still giving her time fillers, but based on her mood), she would have to pick out the picture and write the story for it, on an index card (I bought the largest index cards I could find). It became a beautiful time-filler, absorbing some of that pain, and it still is.

Did you give the child/children time-fillers such as this? If not, what will you do now?

_____
_____
_____
_____
_____
_____
_____
_____
_____
_____
_____
_____
_____
_____
_____

_____
_____
_____
_____

There is another movie that I feel has an element that is most beneficial for kids dealing with loss, this can be for older kids, as well. It is not a cartoon. It is called Blended, starring and produced, by Adam Sandler. I think he did an awesome job with showing how to respecting his grieving children in the movie, in their quest to find their new normal, after they lost their mother. He even went so far, as to leave a chair at the table for his wife, which had passed away, and the children were able to select it, in real time, giving them the comfort of her being there, even though she didn't appear to the human eye. There was even a scene in the movie where his daughter designated a space in the bed for her deceased mother, and he asked if he could lay there, and when the child said, 'Mom is laying there', he said 'I know, I was going to cuddle up to her' and when his child said she didn't want to see that, he selected another spot to sleep in. That made me tear up, as I now will allow Angela to save a seat for her sister, in restaurants and any other place where she _would have_ sat, had she still been physically here. I will do that for Angela until she no longer feels the need to, allowing her to pace her grieving with this little displayed marker. I commend Adam Sandler, for this movie and an awesome portrayal of protecting the hearts of the surviving children. My hat is off to Adam Sandler. ((I would recommend adults _view this movie first_, as it goes further to dealing with blended families, which I think he also did an awesome job on, but I am trying to make sure there are no sensitive issues that applies to your household in this film.)) Adam Sandler, much respect to you dude, on this one.

I hope that you are empowered and encouraged, after reading this book and imparted, with at least hope, that you _can_ save the surviving child/children. All the while, by looking at this book collectively, you will be able to restore your masterpieces, the surviving children's disjointed souls. Every single fragmented beautiful piece, safely framed by _your_ framework.

In fact, to assist you with your plan of action, starting today, allow the child/children, if they are of age to write, to answer the following questions.

Baby, how are you?

_____
_____
_____
_____

I know you are missing your loved one_____. What would you tell them if you could call them on the phone today?

_____
_____
_____
_____
_____
_____
_____
_____
_____
_____
_____
_____
_____

What do you want the world to know about _____?

_____
_____
_____
_____
_____
_____
_____
_____
_____
_____

Close your eyes, remember _____'s smile. How do you want to keep that smile alive? What do you want to do, to show the world that you know how to keep that smile on _____ face?

_____
_____
_____
_____
_____
_____
_____
_____
_____
_____
_____

_____

_____

What do you want to do for _____ that you haven't
been able to do yet? (Send up balloons to heaven, write a letter, in a bottle
dropped off at the ocean, etc.)

_____

_____

_____

_____

_____

_____

_____

_____

_____

_____

_____

What do you want the grown-ups, around you, to know, in order to make
you feel better?

_____

_____

_____

_____

_____

_____

_____

What questions do you have baby?

_____

_____

_____

_____

_____

_____

_____

_____

_____

_____

_____

_____

_____

_____

_____

_____

_____

Either let the child/children write their answers here, or write those questions off, on a sheet of paper. If you didn't have the luxury of this information from the beginning, you still need to know this information now in order to start to impact their healing, going forward. You may think, you don't want to ask these questions, because you don't want to open up their wounds. That is no different than the 'outsiders' that tried to always stop you from crying. Did that make you feel any better? No. You bottled it all in, and to what avail? If you don't open this up for the surviving child/children, how will they get better? If you don't take this lid off of their 'steam pot' of grief, do you think the steam dissipates? No, it only creates added pressure, always. If this pressure has no outlet, in which to release, are you aware that they will continue to burn on the inside? Do you _now_ understand that? What do you think is creating issues, in the life of Bobbi Kristina Brown, the daughter of the late Great Whitney Houston, as we speak? She is on life support, this very day and fighting for her own life, on the 3 year anniversary of the death of her mother. Do you think that is a coincidence? Release the lid! Give the surviving child/children of grief, a fighting chance at a 'new normal', period.

Now today as I write this to you, there is real life story of America's Most Grievous child, playing out in the media right now. America's, not mine, that would be my loving Angela, not yours, because you will now, do the work you learned in this book to save _yours_. But America's child, Bobbi Kristina Brown, the daughter of the legendary late Whitney Houston and Bobby Brown lay in a hospital fighting, actually literally fighting for her life. She is in a medically induced coma. Can I tell you, that _that_ baby girl was in a coma, long before she landed in that hospital? Why? Because all of the adults, in an effort to help her, ushered her to appear to be better, than she actually was. This child was not better. She was not getting any better. Her grief lid was locked on tight. The media, family and friends, all propagated this farce of comfort. Her mother was her everything. She and her mother, The Awesome Iconic Whitney Houston, were together every single day of her life. Now fast forward to 3 years ago, when Bobbi Kristina had her mother ripped from her. All of a sudden there will be no more waking days with her Mommy, ANYMORE. Our beloved Whitney Houston, was and IS Her Mommy. She can't drive anywhere to see her mommy, ANYMORE. She can't pick up a phone and dial any numbers and hear her mommy's voice, ANYMORE. That grieving sorrow-filled baby girl of Whitney & Bobby's has been in agony, completely lost, ever since she lost her Mommy. I wish I could have gifted her family with this book long before now, as I sit here praying that Whitney Houston's baby makes it through this. Whitney Houston's music was a saving grace for me, growing up in the dysfunctional abusive home, I grew up in. Now I only wish I could return the favor, by educating and empowering everyone that is around her mourning baby girl, with their very own copy, of this book. It isn't too late. Just as I am pleading with all of you, it is not too late to help the sad children. We have to save the surviving inconsolable little ones, little but with the biggest pain, they have ever known. It will require that we put in the painstaking work. Don't you see what is at stake? Before your brokenhearted child/children end up in a hospital, like Bobbie Kristina. There will be no help there, as there is no diagnostic test for a broken heart and a severely injured soul. She was thrust and maneuvered into a counterfeit wellbeing status. I am so certain, that everyone around all had the best of intentions, just as we spoke of before.

The point is still the same, intentions are not sufficient, when it comes to these babies. We have to work diligently with premeditated measures and deliberate communications in order to save these surviving children. Like with Bobbi Kristina, she will never be over this loss, but hopefully she can get through much better than she has, if the adults would move deliberately in her shattered world. Just as my sweet Angela will never be over it. But I will use all of my shallow breaths to get her 'Angie' through it and ensure others are controlled, producing an advantageous effect, when it comes to all consolation efforts. You have to pledge today to do the same. It is not too late to save the Surviving Children. Answer their S.O.S.

7. WRITE YOUR OWN CHAPTER

My hope is that this body of work, composed from the deepest parts of my soul, after having lost my 21 year old firstborn, has eased a portion of your pain and the crevices created by the loss of your loved one. As taught by all of the modern day therapeutic philosophical persons, of our time, like the great late Maya Angelou, Iyanla Vanzant, Oprah Winfrey, and Dr. Phil, you now have to look inward, to change any outside situations, including your very own 'new normal'. This chapter is where you will do that. As a grieving Journalist, I will lead you in mapping out and defining your coping navigational skills. Keep your pencil ready, as your answers, may change in time.

Certain things, like perspective, can be most effective, in your healing going forward. Foundational things, like guilt, can impede on your progress, where it should not even exist in the first place. Did you know that there is a substantial difference between powerlessness and things over which you have no control? Sounds simple, doesn't it? But if you have blamed yourself for the unexpected untimeliness of your loved ones death, you may very well be shouldering an encumbrance that is more of a hindrance to your healing, than serving any other purpose. So like with any luggage, it is important to unpack from your previous trip (the experience of your loved one's death), then organize and repack for your next trip (your search, for your 'new normal' post-loss).

The first misconception that you often experience, just as I did, is that if you start a healing process, *any* healing, it somehow means, that you are getting over them or invalidating the love you have for them, and minimizing the effect their death had on you. That is simply not true. Healing is surviving, healing is necessary, to be at a place where you can create and add value, to their continued existence, even after their absence. You can give their past life a new life that is pivotal in helping others. You can touch people after your loved one's death, which neither of your lives would have touch or intersected, during their time here. You have to be, actively seeking a stabilized state, to pull this off, effectively. Let me show you.

First, who did you lose? And who were they to you, if you had to tell the world, here?

_____
_____
_____
_____
_____
_____
_____
_____
_____
_____
_____
_____
_____

When was the last time you spoke to your loved one, and what was your conversation about?

_____
_____
_____
_____
_____
_____
_____
_____
_____
_____
_____

What was your loved one's cause of death?

_____
_____
_____
_____
_____

_____
_____
_____
_____

Who do you blame, if anyone, for your loss?:

_____
_____
_____
_____
_____
_____
_____
_____

How did you find out your loved one had died, who told you?

_____
_____
_____
_____
_____
_____
_____
_____
_____

What were you doing, at the time, of learning of their passing?

_____
_____
_____
_____
_____

_____
_____
_____
_____
_____
_____
_____
_____
_____

Is it something that awareness would have prevented or changed?

_____
_____
_____
_____
_____

What was their age at the time of death?

_____

Who are the top 3 individuals left behind, most affected, by your loved one's death? And why are they the top 3 that are most impacted?

_____
_____
_____
_____
_____
_____
_____
_____
_____

The reason, for this first set of questions, is to take you back, to the actual event and original feelings you were feeling at that devastating time of loss. This is not designed to hurt you. This exercise is to provide you with information that will be utilized, in your quest for your 'new normal', as well as to design a new life, that includes *them* and not just the *grief of losing them*. Now that you are there, we must discern other things that are of actual value, in how you will show your loved one's continued importance to the world, going forward.

Their continued value is not, in the amount of tears you shed, or the days you cannot get out of bed. That is how I felt initially, that is another reason why I wouldn't watch television or laugh or anything that meant that I didn't want her back every single second of every single day. I later learned that their added value will be in how you memorialize them after death. I suggest to you, that by redefining their contribution to the rest of the world, you can live *for* them, now. The manner in which you take their death and give life to others, will be their "STAR", on your tumultuous walk of *their* fame. That is it. That is how you show the world that you, *not only*, will never allow your loved one to be forgotten, but you will campaign the campaign of *how* they are remembered. How does that sound to you?

I can tell you, it has been a saving grace for Tre, Angela, & I. Even though we hurting all the way, but we are not allowing her life to be forgotten, while making the world remember her for the good that we will do in her name. This keeps her solidly in our family, right where she belongs.

You see, being pro-active in a cause, that they are foundationally responsible for is how you keep them remembered. They will also become a part of your everyday life this way. You will not be getting *over* them, you will be giving them life again, by utilizing your life, as sad as you may feel, to impact the lives of others. This won't mean getting *over*, this will mean getting *through*. As my deceased daughter told my surviving son, "DON'T MOVE ON, MOVE UP"!! My gift to the world, in my daughter's name is THE KCA MOVEMENT. The Keep Chelsea Alive Movement, 'The KCA Movement', can be found on Facebook, and I would ask that you stop reading right now and pull up that page and hit LIKE. Also go to www.thekcamovement.com and share our website with others. You will be able to see how my answers to those above questions gave birth to The KCA Movement. You will find your cause, in how you answered the questions in this book, as well as continuing to do your work, with all that you have taken in, from this body of work. Let's continue.

Is there a certain group, of people that their cause of death, impacts, to your knowledge?

_____

_____

_____

_____

_____

_____

_____

Have you researched any groups, such as on Facebook that have this cause, in common, so as to locate support and a network, during your quest?

_____

_____

_____

_____

_____

_____

_____

_____

_____

What have you learned, from other people that share your experience? Or when you share your experience, with people dealing with your similar loss?

_____

_____

_____

_____

_____

_____

_____

_____

_____

_____

_____

_____

Is there anything, in the above answers, that you want the world to know?

_____

_____

_____

_____

_____

_____

_____

_____

_____

_____

_____

_____

_____

Further thoughts to consider, in deciding a cause that will memorialize your loved one can be discerned from your above writing; For example, if it was a car accident, was the absence of seatbelts a factor? Was texting involved? Was alcohol involved, by the other party or your loved one? If it was Breast cancer, could regular mammograms have detected something earlier? Or is there a cause located in the area where you selected your top 3 most affected individuals? For example, is there a fatherless girl *now,* due to your loss?

If their death was the result of a crime, and you did not feel that you got justice, is there something that you wish your local congressmen, were motivated, to change? Like my close dear friend, Phyllis Matthews that lost her 22 year old son, Preston LeShaw Arrington Reed, on November 9, 2014 to gun violence. His Mother or his sister, Kiera Matthews, will never be the same. I am certain that Phyllis did not wake that November day, thinking she would never hug her Preston, again. And now that she has buried her child, she will not allow his life and memories, to stop there. She has even had to endure defamation of her son's memory, by the local media and a retired law official, all while she has yet, to get any type of handle on her loss. She is now circulating a petition, to not allow slander of her sweet boy, *after he was the victim* of a senseless crime. Despite devastation, this cause was thrust in her lap, as she would now battle to preserve the memory of her Dear Preston. Her time will now be filled with fighting for, while living for her son. There are many angles, of your loss that you can be active with now, while searching for your 'new normal'. Some will land in your lap like with Phyllis. If not, by reviewing all that we discussed here, you can identify a worthy cause. This can be a source of consolation, as well an answer, to a portion of your needing to be able to hold onto your loved one, through this newly engineered cause.

You did not choose to be in the spot, that you are in now, but you are the only person that can go on, for them, in the way that they deserve. Write and safely keep this chapter, this book. Re-read it as you need to. Share it with those around you, to give added insight into the steps you are having to take, just to try to take a step. It hurts to have suffered this loss. I hope that from the exercise above you were able to deduce some information that will serve as beneficial, at some point. I hope that you will be able to do the work above, from this momentous event, and derive some motivation and material, with which, to develop a foundation, for the continued legacy of this person that you loved so very much. Just know that you were just as important to them as they were to you. Show them that they still are, in your own time, of course. I hope that this book will assist you, even if, in a minuscule way, to know that you are not alone, with your upcoming journey. I also hope to provide you with encouragement and a template, on the inclusion of your missed loved one, and in a way that can bring you some sense of relief, as well. Even when others around you cannot alleviate your sorrow, your involvement in a cause centered on your missing loved one, will fill some of the canyons of anguish, during this painful journey you have been unhappily, placed on. Your 'new normal' to-do list can start to be identified from writing your own chapter.

8. THE KCA MOVEMENT

The death of my daughter became the epitome of the field testing, of every skill set I have ever possessed.

Every rise, fall, and rise again chant that has ever passed through this skeletal structure. Skeletal not because I am just bones, skeletal because I would have to reference the very infrastructure, of my existence, to formulate this next step, any step, pass HER, pass the passing of HER.

Every tool and weapon, in my carefully selected, meticulously collected, arsenal, of 43 years, came up short. The very manner in which I'd collected this *now* useless weaponry and every piece of ammunition, previously relied upon to attempt victories in life's battles and missions, were all now somehow, gunpowder-free. I'd pull the trigger and aim, at this mission's adversary, my life's largest adversary in fact, the death of my child, and with the canon power I'd called upon before, there would be no canon at all, this time. I pulled for detonation and got the power equivalency of a water-pistol packing the thrust, only enough, to spew pudding.

HOW? 'How', became the operative of reconnaissance, if by chance, any chance, as miniscule of a quantity of a chance, I had to come up out of this one. Nothing prepared me for the loss of my child. The loss of my Firstborn, The loss of my twin, my best friend. How would I progress or move forward, when moving isn't even an option? I had to progress, in the simplest of tasks, no effective weaponry in sight, when breathing wasn't even automatic anymore, for Angie and Tre. I simply had to.

Moving Forward? Past the greatest loss known to mankind? This was not within my scope or grasp. That becomes and became far too paralyzing, as a starting point, from which to calculate. Why? Why would I want to progress? That answer was far simpler to confer and announce. My Son, My Baby girl was the answer to this "why". They would need me. They would need me now. They would need me now, far greater than their beautiful, big humored hearts, ever had before. SHE would count on me, for them. The 'why' was crystal clear. The 'why' was the only absolute, the only certainty, in this anaconda piranha populated muddiest of water, in which I had, to swim, after being dropped here on August 7, 2014.

How would I swim? I knew why, but how? The thing about a loss of this magnitude, it doesn't just erase your happiness, it resets the master switch on your soul. A HARD RESET! All previously saved, stored, and frequently used Apps- GONE! Just GONE! DEFAULT settings-NONE!

There would be no leverage, in this undertaking. My pride and joy was being a mother, a mother of 3 great souls. Even simpler put, it's like having a great set of legs. But that is only possible with the ankle, knee and hip, well my KNEE IS MISSING! Remember? In this simple analogy, a compliment of my lower extremity, is not what I seek, now I am trying, to calculate how to be mobile with missing knees. For those of you, having had a leg injury, you remember the uncomfortableness and the impossibility, at times, of mobility. With an injury, there is definitely no mobility, of any functional speed or ease. Now go back and re-read a couple of sentences ago. My knees are not injured. My knees aren't twisted, fractured, lacerated or broken. MY KNEES ARE MISSING! That is all, I can equate my *potential* mobility to, without my firstborn.

So now the 'how' has melted and dwindled into a big fat whopping, 'IF'. But as soon as the deflating and withering of my desire ensues, the 'why' causes me, to bring my arm forward overhead again, as if in a breaststroke motion and decide to attempt to swim, just a little more, even when treading isn't possible. For them, I have to swim. I would backstroke creature infested waters, for my children, for My Son, for my Baby Girl, For My Firstborn!

The Mother of these 3 children had not been a 'rock wall' climber. The Mother of these 3 children had successfully climbed, to the tiptop peak of 'many a mountains'. She, being me, had overcame so many adversities. Many abrasions and broken bones later, like being raised in an abusive home, yet still excelled in all academics. I'd never completed college, had failed at being married, survived domestic violence, overcame discrimination in corporate America, and still had raised my 3 Children in the absence of any child support or reliable assistance. There had been some assistance I received, from my mother, but even that was severely tainted. My firstborn and niece had been molested, while with family, by my sisters' husband, Reginald Dixon, of Jacksonville Florida and even a decade-plus later, it had been handled so improperly, covered up and disputed, by this supposed family unit leading to heartbreak for me and my firstborn, even up to the end. This betrayal played a key role, even in the date of the death of my firstborn. If you want to know that complete backstory, read SAFE by D.D.T. Gray,(found at www.createspace.com/4969825) My gritty expose' novel, written within the days and weeks following the loss, of My Chelsea. My rage-filled attempt at justice, 122 pages worth.

My mountains, albeit painful, and even with the scars to prove it, all the climbing in years past, were useless in this latest peak.

Just as chronicled in the novel, SAFE by D.D.T. Gray, there were injustices, betrayal, and unfairness that had been out of my control, in protecting my firstborn. For Chelsea, this included bullying by outsiders & family members, body image issues, health issues, as a result of all that she had endured, underage alcohol and drug usage, depression and suicidal tendencies to end the pain. All of these painful elements considered, I was now without my firstborn.

I had died that day too. August 7, 2014 was not just the death of my firstborn, but the death of my parent's baby girl. ME. How would this resemblance of me, which was nothing like me, with this useless arsenal, that was nothing like my arsenal, take on the greatest battle of life, with these hypothetical pudding-filled pistols, I was left with after losing my child?

How? Not, how would I climb this mountain? This mountain was not in front of me. This mountain had landed atop of me.

I lacked perspicacity, problem solving, or desire, without her. I lacked the strength to lift a pebble, so 'How' do I dare rise, to this latest life-altering, heart-shredding challenge? But here were the facts. This mountain was also bearing down, on the beings of My Son and My Baby girl. I would have to. I would have to move it, simply because they are under this life-crushing weight. I'd simply have to get them out, up, or at least, in an aptitude, to breathe. I'd have to find a way, 'knee-less' legs and all, to stand. All the while, never knowing even if I could, just simply knew for them, I had to.

Mentally resolute that I could never put a check mark on my to-do list, next to 'Move Mountain', I knew this would take the remainder of my lifetime. The attempting of this feat, would have to commence though. Emotionally, I premeditated I'd never complete it, but I have to get air to my boy and my baby girl, somehow.

All I wanted was HER back; My 3 pack complete. How could I have my set complete again? I carried and gave birth to and loved immensely, 3 children.

Thinking isn't an option. There is no alternative, containing selection where I will ever choose 2. I will always knowingly, unknowingly, intentionally, unintentionally, inbred, innately pick 3, My 3, my perfect triangle, of Love and being. I have to have all 3 of them. ALIVE. That is the answer to my most painful 'HOW'. I have to save them, by keeping all 3, of them, alive. Chelsea isn't just MY Chelsea, SHE is HIS, Tre's, Chelsea. SHE is HERS, Angela's Chelsea too. SHE is our Chelsea. I can save them, by keeping our Chelsea Alive. So in death, lies my defeat, lies all 3, of our defeats. I can't let them be defeated. That isn't an option for me. For THEM, I have to Keep Chelsea Alive. Thus after my own death, in every other sense of the word, minus a burial plot, The KEEP CHELSEA ALIVE MOVEMENT is Born!

The Keep Chelsea Alive Movement, fondly called, The KCA Movement is here. For them, all 3 of them, I had to create an honor worthy of the Beautiful Chelsea Alexis and the value she provided to Tre, Angela and I. I can't leave my niece, Tavia, out here, as she was a portion, of my motivation as well, as she had never known life, without her cousin. They were more like sisters than cousins, their entire lives. Chelsea also had a cast of friends that depended on her, for advice and support, as she was so unselfish. She would help everyone even when she couldn't help and save herself. She had made her mark. In an overwhelming amount of pain from all that she endured, some known, most unbeknownst to me, she was still the source for smiles in a lot of people's lives. I couldn't let the world, our world go on without her.

If you go to www.thekcamovement.com, you will see our cause we started, in her name, is designed to do so much good, for all other young people, with like experiences of Chelsea's. We will reach out, to all youth in crisis, rather they have experienced bullying, body image issues, mental health issues, past molestation or sexual abuse, divided family issues, and any other crisis that they youth are subjected to. The KCA Movement will provide a network of solutions and an empowerment platform geared to facilitate these youthful future leaders with additional outlooks, perspectives, and solutions to enhance their lives, despite calamity.

The KCA Movement, will work diligently to form alliances with the school system, so as to reach all middle school, high school, and college students, before they choose, to allow despair, to overcome their opportunities. We won't allow them, to succumb to giving up on or ending their lives, instead we will be empowering them, to enhance it. We will assure them that they are not alone, through relatable presentations, concerts, materials, and networks of supporters of The KCA Movement. The movement is geared for fortifying the youth, while they are undertaking these trials and tribulations that they face, sometimes and mostly, unbeknownst, to the very adults that are closest to them.

The KCA Movement is how I will keep her remembered after death, appropriately worthy of who she was to us when she lived. Which she will always live, living everyday in our lives through The KCA Movement. Go to www.thekcamovement.com and show your love and support, just as I will do when you design your cause for your loved one. We will be able to go on, never getting over, but getting through with the work of, the one and only, The KCA Movement!

8. DEAR DIARY

Dear Diary,   2-13-15

Today is February 13, 2015. To the world it is Friday the 13th. Funny to me how everyone sees Friday the 13th. After losing my child, it is as if my calendar read August 7, 2014, the next day Friday the 13th, the day after that Friday the 13th, and every other day all the way up to this one, Friday the 13th, per my calendar. Yours doesn't read the same way? Friday the 13th, would be one of the only days on your regular calendar that equates to my days every single day. A day, per the world, associated with fear and experiences of bad luck, is that not what every day is for me after 8/7/14? The worst luck and only fearing that I will never wake up from this nightmare, all the while, saying that with my eyes wide open. Is that not the most horrific frightful thing ever? The world doesn't even know that I no longer have phobias. I can't possible have any fear of the regularly feared things, on this day, as all of my worst fears, have already came true. Do you realize the implications here? My worst, absolute unequivocal wickedest fear, already came and passed. That, I can only attribute to experiencing a pain like I'd never known, all the while, my eyes still wide open, engorged to the point of vision obstruction, but open for this nightmare. So Friday the 13th you say? Day of frightfulness, creepiness, and fear factors? The overcast of this day is wasted on me. This will probably be my most normal day, if you were tracking my whereabouts, through usage of a calendar or time marking device. I am only sickened knowing that tomorrow is coming. Tomorrow, Valentine's Day for you. The Happy Valentine's Day, for you, that is. No Happy anything for me.

My Holidays are HOLLOW-DAYS!!

Dear Diary,

February 14, 2015. Here they go. The world rejoicing. I can't. I can't say Happy Anything. Even with all of their Valentines wishes and poems and picturesque red hearts, they are screaming HAPPY Valentine's Day. I am thankful for any of their acknowledgments, but I wont even say 'you too' to any of their posts or messages containing the word HAPPY.

Just like Christmas, I will give this one back to them as well. I don't need it to express my love to Tre or my love to Angela. I tell them every day and show them each and every chance I get with whatever my fragmented soul has left. I can't join them in their HAPPY intro's to things or these days they consider special, still. Yes still. I actually expected the world to stop with this merriment after you left, or at least my soul, Tre soul, Angela soul stopped celebrating their festivities their way after August 7, 2014. I know this, because just as last night was Friday the 13th, I started that day of fear for them, with Tre outpouring his heart in his latest song KCA MEMORIES. They will understand after they hear that song, that we are not marking our calendars with any of their festivities. Just don't seem festivity is possible without you, unless it is about you. Chelsea You Are our EVERYTHING!!

I did what you asked me and tried to gift the world with this body of work, Chelt. I hope that I made you proud. I will smile a little today. Their day of Valentines, will be a day that shows my love for you and your love for me, even across the galaxies. How so, the world may ask?? She loved me enough to impart me with this task. She cared enough for you, to force me to do it, at a time that she knew I had no idea of how I would survive- The Holidays, without her. I love her enough to live long enough to attempt to complete it, the task *she* gave me. Ironically, on this day of LOVE, I can tell her, that even though we are worlds apart, I could wrap and now present to my Universal Love Chelsea, this book, My First Christmas. Chelt', I hope I made you smile. I won't stop trying to making you proud. Tre won't stop making you proud. Angela won't stop making you proud. We LOVE YOU SO VERY MUCH!!

Without YOU, My Holidays will always be HOLLOW DAYS!

64258703R00057

Made in the USA
Lexington, KY
02 June 2017